*J*UMPTUOUS DESSERTS
THE SLIM CUISINE WAY

Other cookbooks published by Consumer Reports Books

SLIM CUISINE
by Sue Kreitzman

THE INCREDIBLE POTATO COOKBOOK
by Maria Luisa Scott and Jack Denton Scott

GOOD EATING, GOOD HEALTH COOKBOOK
by Phyllis C. Kaufman

THE BEAN, PEA, AND LENTIL COOKBOOK
by Maria Luisa Scott and Jack Denton Scott

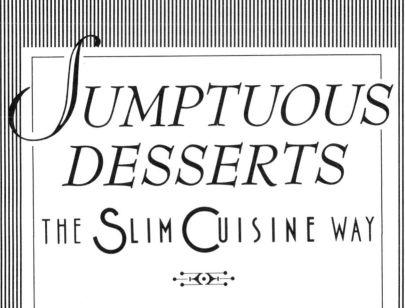

SUMPTUOUS DESSERTS
THE SLIM CUISINE WAY

SUE KREITZMAN
AND THE EDITORS OF
CONSUMER REPORTS BOOKS

CONSUMER REPORTS BOOKS
A DIVISION OF CONSUMERS UNION
Yonkers, New York

Copyright © 1993 by Sue Kreitzman
Published by Consumers Union of United States, Inc.,
Yonkers, New York 10703.
All rights reserved, including the right
of reproduction in whole or in part in any form.
Library of Congress Cataloging-in-Publication Data
Kreitzman, Sue.
Sumptuous desserts the slim cuisine way / by Sue Kreitzman and the
editors of Consumer Reports Books.—1st American ed.
p. cm.
Rev. ed. of: Slim cuisine desserts.
Includes index.
ISBN 0-89043-577-4
1. Reducing diets—Recipes. 2. Low-calorie diets—Recipes.
3. Low-fat diets—Recipes. 4. Desserts. I. Kreitzman, Sue. Slim
cuisine desserts. II. Consumer Reports Books. III. Title.
RM222.2.K72 1993
641.8'6—dc20 *92-41653*
CIP

Photographs by Sue Atkinson
China used courtesy of Token House-Windsor
Design by Ruth Kolbert
First printing, April 1993
Manufactured in the United States of America

Sumptuous Desserts the Slim Cuisine Way is a Consumer Reports Book published by Consumers Union, the nonprofit organization that publishes *Consumer Reports,* the monthly magazine of test reports, product Ratings, and buying guidance. Established in 1936, Consumers Union is chartered under the Not-For-Profit Corporation Law of the State of New York.

The purposes of Consumers Union, as stated in its charter, are to provide consumers with information and counsel on consumer goods and services, to give information on all matters relating to the expenditure of the family income, and to initiate and to cooperate with individual and group efforts seeking to create and maintain decent living standards.

Consumers Union derives its income solely from the sale of *Consumer Reports* and other publications. In addition, expenses of occasional public service efforts may be met, in part, by nonrestrictive, noncommercial contributions, grants, and fees. Consumers Union accepts no advertising or product samples and is not beholden in any way to any commercial interest. Its Ratings and reports are solely for the use of the readers of its publications. Neither the Ratings, nor the reports, nor any Consumers Union publication, including this book, may be used in advertising or for any commercial purpose. Consumers Union will take all steps open to it to prevent such uses of its material, its name, or the name of *Consumer Reports.*

*For my dear
chocolate-loving friends,
Margaret and Terry Pedersen*

CONTENTS

ACKNOWLEDGMENTS

Many, many thanks to my secretary, Rosemarie Espley, and to my assistant, Sandie Mitchel-King. Thanks as well to their families, who were always willing to taste an unlimited number of new Slim Cuisine desserts, and then give the recipes the thumbs up or thumbs down. Thanks, too, to helper Brenda Huebler, whose hard work ensures that we do not become mired in chaos. Brenda's family also served as intrepid tasters, and Brenda contributed a recipe of her own, Strawberry Frozen Yogurt. And thank you to helper Mary Hardy, who is, by now, practically a member of the family.

I am deeply grateful to Howard Foundation Research for their support of my research, and to my husband, Dr. Stephen Kreitzman. Under the tutelage of Dr. Husband, I have been able to breathe the rarefied air of international obesity research.

Alison Campbell at Panasonic has been generous with advice

on the role of the microwave in dessert cookery, and was kind enough to loan me a machine for testing purposes.

Sue Atkinson, with the help of Carol Handslip, produced a set of photographs that outstripped even her usual brilliant efforts; I am in awe of her ability to give my recipes such pulsating and vivid photographic life.

Margaret and Terry Pedersen have—as always—been helpful, enthusiastic, and supportive. And Margaret, and the Nutran analysis program, provided all the nutritional analysis for each recipe. Her efforts are greatly appreciated.

And to my son Shawm, who thinks that Slim Cuisine Chocolate Sorbet is one of life's ultimates, thanks for making *my* life so interesting.

INTRODUCTION

Dessert figures strongly in memories of childhood's golden moments. In my travels, whenever I ask people to share recipes and food memories with me (and I do ask—tirelessly), the subject of dessert comes up again and again. All over the world, people reminisce with deep fondness about sweet things that were served to them in childhood by a mother, grandmother, or aunt. Whether it is the custard-soaked, raisin-studded voluptuousness of an English bread pudding, the legendary velvet creaminess of a New York cheesecake, the supernal comfort of a hot fudge sundae, the mashed bread-and-berry juiciness of a scarlet summer pudding, or the milky sweetness of a noodle pudding, it is inevitably described with an almost tearful intensity.

For those who can feel themselves ballooning at the mere mention of cream, butter, eggs, and excess sugar, and for those who have enlightened views on diet and health, dessert nostalgia can be a nightmare. Are fat-prone adults doomed to suffer? When we choose the desserts of yesteryear, do we also choose ill health and obesity?

Some weight control "experts" say, "Eat small portions only." What nonsense! Small portions are agonizing—and what *is* a small portion? Fat people (and ex–fat people) have trouble defining this concept. By the time we finish weighing and measuring and scrutinizing, any joy we may have gleaned from our pitiful serving is gone. And with the tastes and textures of that small serving lingering on our palates and in our minds, how do we spend the rest of the evening, knowing the remainder waits in its dish, sending out seductive messages that only we seem to hear?

Others say "Don't eat desserts at all—have a piece of underripe fruit instead." Even worse, "Eat this beautiful cheesecake, specially constructed for you from tofu and saccharine, or this 'chocolate' mousse fabricated from carob and powdered egg whites."

Give me a break! Save me from the thin advisers. It's true that I'm determined to protect my health, and *never be fat again,* but I still want lavishness, deep taste, and excitement in my culinary encounters. This desire has impelled me to attempt to "reinvent" desserts. I have thrown out many of the basics, dependent as they are (and have been for centuries) on fats and oils. New techniques had to be developed to ensure that the food is not insipid. I am determined to maintain flavor and culinary interest. Why shouldn't low-fat desserts be as sumptuous, delicious, and seductive as the old-fashioned high-fat ones?

What fun I've had applying this criteria to desserts and other sweet things, especially those fraught with nostalgia. Slim Cuisine cheese pies, for instance, are creamy, with a crunchy base—they put many conventional killer cheesecakes to shame. Rice pudding, ice cream, towering cakes, pies, flans, tortes, chocolate pudding . . . I'm talking total delight here. And—believe it—not a speck of carob, not a dollop of tofu in sight. These desserts are the real thing. They taste wonderful, but they all contribute significantly to a healthy, very low-fat life-style. Enjoy!

SOME FACTS ABOUT INGREDIENTS

FAT

Using the concepts of Slim Cuisine will allow you to eat splendidly without overloading on fat. All the recipes in this book use no added fat: no butter, oil, lard, margarine, solid vegetable shortening, or any other type of pure fat. Whole eggs, with their fatty high-cholesterol yolks, have been kept to a minimum, and high-fat nuts are almost never used. Cream or other whole milk dairy products have been avoided as well. Producing gorgeous desserts *without* these traditional killer ingredients has been one of the most exhilarating challenges of my professional career. I now know I can have my cake (and my pie and ice cream and bread pudding) and I can keep my slim figure too. Because the fat dimension is missing from these recipes and the empty sugar Calories have been cut back, their Calorie levels have been drastically reduced. Remember, fat weighs in at 100 to 120 Calories per tablespoon (more than twice the Calories, gram for gram, of carbohydrate or protein). What's more, fat is metabolized differently from carbohydrate and protein; it goes directly to the body's fat stores with heartbreaking efficiency. A very low fat content means that you automatically save hundreds (sometimes thousands) of the most fattening kind of Calories.

SUGAR

Once, not too many years ago, sugar was blamed for a bewildering host of human ailments, from blindness to heart disease, from tooth decay to extreme depression, from diabetes to gallstones. Since those days, the scientific wind has changed direction and sugar paranoia is no longer with us. Tooth decay is about the only problem laid at sugar's door these days, and even that is tempered with common sense. Frequency of carbohydrate consumption, texture, and food particle size are factors that seem to play a major role in the production of dental decay.

So far as overweight is concerned, fat, at 9 Calories per gram, is much more of a problem than sugar is at 4. And, as mentioned before, fat Calories are metabolized in such a way that they do, literally, make you fatter faster than the Calories from protein or carbohydrate. Still, sugar's 4 Calories per gram are "empty" Calories—that is, sugar provides food energy (Calories) and nothing else. As a result, sugar should be used intelligently. The natural sugar you consume in fresh fruits and vegetables works in concert with the valuable nutrients (vitamins, minerals, trace minerals, and fiber) found in those fruits and vegetables, so that the foodstuff is both highly nutritious *and* delicious. Take a tip from nature and use sugar *sparingly* in your recipes while also using as many valuable nutrients as possible. Nutrient density coupled with lovely flavor is what good cooking is all about.

Brown sugars, unrefined sugars, and honey are no more nutritious than plain white sugar. It's true that unrefined sugar and honey contain tiny amounts of vitamins and minerals while white sugar contains none at all, but the operant word here is *tiny*. Unrefined sugar and honey would have to be consumed in enormous quantities in order for their traces of nutrients to contribute significantly to daily requirements. For instance, it would take more than 7½ cups of honey (8,000 Calories worth) to come close to meeting a woman's daily requirement for riboflavin.

That is not to say that the fat-prone person should avoid honey at all costs. It has a lovely taste and sweetens beautifully; in fact, it is sweeter than white sugar and so can be used in slightly smaller quantities. Just remember: honey is essentially just another form of sugar, and as such contains virtually empty Calories. Use it with prudence. And if you are trying to *lose* weight, as opposed to maintaining, cut out sugars (including honey) altogether.

LOW-CALORIE SUGAR SUBSTITUTES

Unfortunately, some sugar substitutes cannot be used successfully in baked desserts, or in any dessert that needs to be cooked. They do not react in baking the way sugar does, and when heated, most of their sweetness dissipates. They are extremely useful, however, in ice creams, sorbets, cold dessert sauces, milkshakes, and so on. If you want to *lose* weight, stick to recipes that use low-Calorie sweetener. When you are *maintaining*, you may use sugar some of the time, and a low-Calorie sweetener some of the time. It is never a good idea to overload on either one.

VANILLA

The lovely aroma and flavor of natural vanilla are essential to many of the recipes in this collection. Use vanilla in one of the following ways:

Bottled vanilla extract. Don't ever buy imitation vanilla flavoring; it is harsh and unpleasant.
Vanilla beans. The vanilla bean is the fruit of an orchid, *vanilla planifolia.* You can buy the long, thin, black pods in jars (one per jar) from the herb and spice shelf in many supermarkets. If you slit open the vanilla pod lengthwise with a sharp paring knife you will see (and smell) that it is filled with a hauntingly aromatic pulp. Scrape out the black pulp with the tip of your knife and use it in ice creams, custards, and puddings of all sorts. *Do not* throw away the scraped bean! Use it for vanilla sugar and vanilla low-Calorie sweetener (see below).

Vanilla low-Calorie sweetener and vanilla sugar. Bury a whole vanilla bean or scraped out vanilla bean in a jar of granulated low-Calorie sweetener or a canister of sugar. After a few days, the sweetener will be imbued with the vanilla flavor. When the sweeteners are used up, save the bean. It will last for many jars of low-Calorie sweetener or canisters of sugar.

AMARETTI COOKIES

Amaretti cookies are crunchy almond-flavored meringues from Italy. They can be bought in pretty red and white canisters. When the cookies are gone, the containers are useful for storage. Amaretti, although almond-flavored, contain no high-fat almonds; the flavor comes from apricot kernels. The cookies are very useful in crumb crusts, and in recipes where you want both almond flavor and crunch. They make a good garnish, too. Try them crumbled onto servings of Slim Cuisine Food Processor Ice Creams (page 120). Find amaretti cookies in specialty food shops, Italian delis, and the gourmet food sections of major supermarkets and department stores.

ALCOHOL

When alcohol (wine, spirits, liqueur) is boiled briskly, most of the alcohol (and the alcohol Calories) evaporates. In all recipes in this collection that contain small amounts of alcohol, the alcohol is optional. Depending on the recipe, it can either be omitted or replaced with fruit juice if desired.

DAIRY PRODUCTS

To switch from fat cuisine to Slim Cuisine, you must change your supermarket strategy. On the Slim Cuisine regimen there are certain things you *do not* buy: butter, margarine, "low-fat" spreads, cream, sour cream, full-fat, or semiskim milk, indeed, any full-fat dairy product. Fortunately, there are many excellent skim milk products available; simply get into the habit of buying them instead of the old fat cuisine ingredients. Here is a list of the things to look for; they appear again and again in the Slim Cuisine dessert recipes.

SKIM MILK   It is very easy to switch your palate from whole milk to skim milk. For the first day or so, the skim version may seem a bit thin, but after a week—if you then try to go back to whole or semiskim versions—you will find that the fat in the milk is obtrusive. It coats the tongue and when added to coffee or tea floats in globules on the surface. Give yourself a week to break the full-fat habit—it's easier than you think.

NONFAT DRY MILK   In experimenting with very low-fat desserts, I found that augmenting skim milk with additional nonfat milk powder imparts a wonderful richness to ice creams, bread puddings, and other desserts where a perception of creaminess is important. It adds an extra dimension of calcium and protein as well.

SKIM MILK YOGURT   Read the label. Although many yogurts are labeled low-fat, some are actually only *part* skim. Buy yogurts that contain less than 1 percent fat.

NONFAT COTTAGE CHEESE   Despite the lumps, cottage cheese can be quite useful. In fact, if you whirl it in the processor or blender, the lumps will vanish and the texture will become very creamy (it takes longer in the processor than in the blender). As with all dairy products, *read the label* and buy the cheese that contains less than 1 percent fat. The low-fat cottage cheeses that contain no fillers (guar gum, locust bean gum, and so on) have a lovely fresh taste and work well in Slim Cuisine recipes.

RICOTTA CHEESE Lately, there has been a profusion of lower fat ricotta cheeses available in supermarkets across the country. As with cottage cheeses, the ricottas that contain no fillers and additives are the ones that taste best and work well in recipes. Look for the "light" ricottas that contain only part-skim milk, fresh whey, and cheese culture or starter.

QUARK The word *quark* (in addition to meaning a subatomic particle that only a physicist could know) is an old German word for curd; therefore, quark is a no-fat, beautifully creamy curd cheese, almost like a no-fat cream cheese. It is delicious spread on bread, toast, and bagels, and very versatile in all sorts of lovely recipes (particularly low-fat cheesecakes). A very good quality American quark is being produced by a dairy in the state of Washington and is available in specialty food shops and farmers' markets around the country. If you can find it, I think it will delight you.

BUTTERMILK Real buttermilk is the liquid left over from making butter. It is fat free, because all the butterfat has gone into the butter. The cultured nonfat buttermilk that you buy in the store is not the real thing—it is a beautifully creamy cultured skim milk product. What a wonderful baking ingredient it is, and how valuable for making Slim Cuisine Food Processor Ice Creams (page 120). I find the slightly tart creaminess of cultured buttermilk similar in flavor to the best sour cream. Buy buttermilk, and if—as some brands do—it contains little flakes of butter, strain them out.

FROMAGE BLANC Sometimes called *fromage frais, fromage blanc* is a delicious European dairy product. *Fromage blanc* can be made entirely of skim milk, and so can be entirely fat free. Although it is called *fromage* (cheese) it is not particularly cheeselike; it is more like sour cream or crème fraîche in taste and texture. Like quark, low-fat *fromage blanc,* produced by local independent dairies, is now available in some American supermarkets and specialty food shops.

EGGS

Egg yolks are high in fat and cholesterol, but egg whites are virtually fat free and an excellent source of high-quality protein. Despite the fat, an egg is a nice package of nutrition. If your blood cholesterol levels are high or you have a history of cardiac or arterial problems, you should consume no egg yolks at all, but you may use as many whites as you please in your cookery. Otherwise an occasional whole egg—yolk and all—would be no problem. Current thinking suggests, however, that you do not consume more than three to four a week.

SYMBOLS USED IN THIS BOOK

♡ A recipe flagged with a heart indicates that the dish is low in added sugar as well as very low in fat, and is suitable for a weight *loss* regimen. Recipes without hearts are suitable for Slim Cuisine weight maintenance. Some recipes are followed by instructions for ♡ variations.

🕔 A recipe flagged with a clock indicates that it can be prepared very quickly.

❄ A snowflaked recipe is suitable for freezing.

❖ This symbol indicates that a microwave is needed to prepare the recipe.

A Dose of Nostalgia

BREAD PUDDING

Talk about nostalgia! Soft, creamy, custardy puddings conjure up childhood like nothing else. Rice pudding, noodle pudding, bread pudding . . . they operate as a kind of edible time machine, propelling the pudding eater back to an earlier, less complicated time of life. The most nostalgic of all, I believe, is bread pudding. Mention bread pudding to some folks, and they go all soft and dreamy.

There is *nothing* quite like a good bread pudding. It's the voluptuous texture of the custard-soaked bread, baked so that, ideally, the pudding mysteriously combines delicacy and substance in each sweet mouthful. I've seen recipes for "lighter" bread puddings made with less bread, but lots more butter and eggy, creamy custard. Such formulas don't interest me: they cut back on the beautiful complex carbohydrate (bread) and pile on the fat. They don't taste quite right either.

THE INCONSISTENCY OF OVENS

Before tackling any oven-baked dish in this book, stop for a moment and consider your oven. Several things affect its performance: Is it a convection oven? Is it small or large? Electric or gas? Is its thermostat working properly? Are you baking one thing alone, or several at a time? All of these things affect the cooking time of a recipe. Learn to know your oven. Because ovens differ, you must take the baking time listed in any recipe as an approximation. If a recipe suggests 15 minutes, your oven may need as little as 10 or as much as 20. Always use your first time out with a recipe as a test drive—note the cooking time needed, so you won't have to guess next time around. It is also important to note that most ovens are uneven. During baking, it is a good idea to turn cake pans, or if more than one thing is baking, switch their shelf positions halfway through.

A good, nostalgic bread pudding should not levitate off the tongue like a soufflé. Instead, it should linger for a moment or two, and *then* it should levitate. I've found that a glorious bread pudding can be produced utilizing *no* fat at all, not even egg yolks. I can hardly even write about it without wanting to rush into the kitchen to whip one up at once.

To ensure perfection in your bread puddings, follow these rules:

1. Use a good quality low-fat or nonfat bakery bread that has been allowed to stand for a day or so out of its bag.
2. After combining the bread with the custard, refrigerate it for a few hours or overnight, so that the bread is thoroughly soaked with the custard mixture. Don't leave it to soak longer or the pudding will be wet and soggy.
3. Always bake the bread pudding in a hot water bath. The pudding dish should rest in a larger baking dish containing boiling water.
4. A bread pudding is a substantial dish; in fact, I always think it is too substantial to be a dessert, unless it follows a truly paltry meal. Why not have a bread pudding as a meal in itself—breakfast, lunch, light supper? In addition to tasting terrific, my bread puddings provide a lovely package of nutrients. They stand beautifully on their own.

Banana Bread Pudding

S E R V E S 6

Per serving: 263.5 Cal. / 0 g fat / 0% fat / 1.71 mg cholesterol

I ask myself, How can something made from stale bread, skim milk, and egg whites taste so outrageously good? The basic ingredients sound austere, but when mixed with ripe bananas, rum, and orange juice, they form an unforgettable bread pudding.

1 tablespoon rum
2 to 3 tablespoons raisins
1 teaspoon vanilla extract
6 ounces one- to two-day-old unsliced low-fat or nonfat
   bakery white bread
1 pound ripe bananas (3 medium), peeled and sliced
½ to ¾ cup fresh orange juice
5 egg whites
5 tablespoons light brown sugar
2 cups skim milk
3 tablespoons nonfat dry milk

1. Combine the rum, raisins, and vanilla extract and let raisins soak.

2. Cut bread into ¾- to 1-inch chunks. Put them in a 12-by-7-inch glass or ceramic baking dish. Mix in the peeled, sliced bananas and orange juice.

3. Beat together the egg whites and sugar. Gently beat in the skim and dry milk and rum-raisin mixture. Pour the mixture over the bread. Use a broad spatula to push the bread into the liquid. Stir it gently, being careful not to break up the bread cubes. Cover the dish and refrigerate for several hours or overnight.

4. Remove the dish from the refrigerator and let stand at room temperature while you preheat the oven to 350° F. Put the kettle on to boil.

5. Choose a baking dish larger than the one with the bread and place it in the preheated oven. Put the smaller dish into the larger one, and pour boiling water in the larger dish to come about halfway up the sides of the smaller one. Bake 30 to 40 minutes, until puffed and firm. (A knife inserted near the center will emerge clean.)

6. Cool the bread pudding on a rack. Serve warm or at room temperature.

Pineapple Bread Pudding

S E R V E S 6
Per serving: 236.3 Cal. / 0 g fat / 0% fat / 1.71 mg cholesterol

Low-fat bread puddings are wonderful when dressed up with liqueurs and with fresh, dried, or canned fruit (don't turn up your nose at canned fruit; it is an excellent, versatile, and convenient foodstuff). This version contains crushed pineapple and a splash of dark rum; if preparing it for children, by all means omit the rum.

> 6 ounces one- to two-day-old unsliced low-fat or nonfat
>   bakery white or whole wheat bread
> One 20-ounce can crushed pineapple in natural juice
> 5 egg whites
> 6 tablespoons light brown sugar
> 2 cups skim milk
> 3 tablespoons nonfat dry milk
> 1 tablespoon dark rum
> 1 teaspoon vanilla extract
> 2 to 3 tablespoons raisins
> Grated rind of ½ orange

1. Cut bread into ¾- to 1-inch chunks. Put them in a 12-by-7-inch glass or ceramic baking dish together with the crushed pineapple and its juices.
2. Beat the egg whites with 5 tablespoons of the sugar. Gently beat in the skim and dry milk and the remaining ingredients except for the remaining brown sugar. Pour the mixture over the bread. Use a broad spatula to push the bread into the liquid. Stir it gently, being careful not to break up the bread cubes. Sprinkle the remaining tablespoon of brown sugar evenly over the top. Cover the dish and refrigerate for several hours or overnight.

||||||||||||||||||||||||||||||||||||||||||||||||||||||||||||||||||||||||

3. Remove the dish from the refrigerator and let stand at room temperature while you preheat the oven to 350° F. Put the kettle on to boil.

4. Choose a baking dish larger than the one with the bread and place it in the preheated oven. Put the smaller dish into the larger one, and pour boiling water in the larger dish to come about halfway up the sides of the smaller one. Bake 30 to 40 minutes, until puffed, browned, and firm. (A knife inserted near the center will emerge clean.)

5. Cool the bread pudding on a rack. Serve warm or at room temperature.

Bread Pudding with Cherries

SERVES 6

Per serving: 199.2 Cal. / 0.92 g fat / 4% fat / 1.33 mg cholesterol

Halved fresh cherries nestling in the custardy bread provide lovely flashes of scarlet. The touch of almond extract complements the fresh cherry flavor.

> 6 ounces one- to two-day-old unsliced low-fat or nonfat bakery white or whole wheat bread
> 5 egg whites
> 3 to 4 tablespoons superfine sugar
> 2 cups skim milk
> 3 tablespoons nonfat dry milk
> 1 teaspoon vanilla extract
> 1 teaspoon almond extract
> Pinch or two of ground cinnamon (optional)
> 1 pound fresh cherries, pitted and halved, or 1-pound bag unsweetened frozen pitted cherries (do not thaw)
> ½ cup fresh orange juice

1. Cut bread into ¾- to 1-inch chunks. Put them in a 12-by-7-inch glass or ceramic baking dish.
2. Beat the egg whites with the sugar. Gently beat in the milk, nonfat dry milk, and flavorings. Pour the mixture over the bread. Use a broad spatula to push the bread into the liquid. Add the cherries and the juice. Stir it all up gently, being careful not to break up the bread cubes. Cover the dish and refrigerate for several hours or overnight.
3. Remove the dish from the refrigerator and let stand at room temperature while you preheat the oven to 350° F. Put the kettle on to boil.
4. Choose a baking dish larger than the one with the bread and place it in the preheated oven. Put the smaller dish in the larger dish, and pour boiling water in the larger dish to come about halfway up the sides of the smaller one. Bake 30 to 40 minutes, until puffed and firm. (A knife inserted near the center will emerge clean.)
5. Cool the bread pudding on a rack. Serve warm or at room temperature.

Bread Pudding with Mincemeat

SERVES 6

Per serving: 351.2 Cal. / 3.00 g fat / 8% fat / 138.33 mg cholesterol

Originally mincemeat actually contained minced meat and suet. The Slim Cuisine mincemeat used in this recipe (see Mincemeat Coffee Cake), is pure fruit. Because this particular pudding contains whole eggs, it is not for those with high blood cholesterol levels.

6 ounces one- to two-day-old unsliced low-fat or nonfat
  bakery white bread
2 egg whites
3 eggs
3½ to 4 tablespoons superfine sugar
2 cups skim milk
1 teaspoon vanilla extract
Pinch or two of ground cinnamon or mixed spice (to taste)
1½ cups mincemeat for Mincemeat Coffee Cake (page 86)

1.   Cut bread into ¾- to 1-inch chunks. Put them in a 12-
by-7-inch glass or ceramic baking dish.
2.   Beat the egg whites and the eggs with the sugar. Beat in
the milk and flavorings. Stir in the mincemeat. Pour the mixture over the bread. Use a broad spatula to push the bread
into the liquid. Stir it all gently, being careful not to break
up the bread cubes. Cover the dish and refrigerate for several
hours or overnight.
3.   Remove the dish from the refrigerator and let stand at
room temperature while you preheat the oven to 350° F. Put
the kettle on to boil.
4.   Choose a baking dish larger than the one with the bread
and place it in the preheated oven. Put the smaller dish in the
larger one, and pour boiling water in the larger dish to come
about halfway up the sides of the smaller one. Bake 30 to 40
minutes, until puffed and firm. (A knife inserted near the
center will emerge clean.)
5.   Cool the bread pudding on a rack. Serve warm or at
room temperature.

Pear Bread Pudding

SERVES 6
Per serving: 273.2 Cal. / 0 g fat / 0% fat / 1.71 mg cholesterol

It's a good idea to keep a selection of canned fruits in their natural (unsweetened) juices in the pantry. It can be a blessing when you are out of the fresh stuff. In this pudding, the texture of the pears works beautifully against the custardy bread.

> 6 ounces one- to two-day-old unsliced low-fat or nonfat
>   bakery white or whole wheat bread
> Two 16-ounce cans pears in natural juice, quartered
> ½ to ¾ cup juice from pears
> 5 egg whites
> 6 tablespoons light brown sugar
> 2 cups skim milk
> 3 tablespoons nonfat dry milk
> 1 tablespoon orange brandy
> 1 teaspoon vanilla extract
> 2 to 3 tablespoons raisins
> Grated rind of ½ orange

1.   Cut bread into ¾- to 1-inch chunks. Put them in a 12-by-7-inch glass or ceramic baking dish, together with the quartered pears and the pear juice.
2.   Beat the egg whites with 5 tablespoons of the sugar. Gently beat in the skim and dry milk and the remaining ingredients except for the remaining brown sugar. Pour the mixture over the bread. Use a broad spatula to push the bread into the liquid. Stir it gently, being careful not to break up the bread cubes. Sprinkle the remaining tablespoon of brown sugar evenly over the top. Cover the dish and refrigerate for several hours or overnight.

||||||||||||||||||||||||||||||||||||||||||||||||||||||||||||||||||||||||||||||||||||||

3.   Remove the dish from the refrigerator and let stand at room temperature while you preheat the oven to 350° F. Put the kettle on to boil.

4.   Choose a baking dish larger than the one with the bread and place it in the preheated oven. Put the smaller dish in the larger one, and pour boiling water in the larger dish to come about halfway up the sides of the smaller one. Bake 30 to 40 minutes, until puffed and firm. (A knife inserted near the center will emerge clean.)

5.   Cool the bread pudding on a rack. Serve warm or at room temperature.

Orange-Lychee Bread Pudding

SERVES 6

Per serving: 257.3 Cal / 0.28 g fat / 1% fat / 1.71 mg cholesterol

I would say that this is my all-time best bread pudding. As with all bread puddings in this collection, it would make a beautiful sweet meal on its own: breakfast, afternoon tea, or light supper.

> 6 ounces one- to two-day-old unsliced low-fat or nonfat bakery white or whole wheat bread
> One 15-ounce can lychees in natural juice
> One 11-ounce can mandarin oranges in natural juice
> ½ cup juice drained from oranges
> 1 tablespoon finely diced crystallized ginger (use scissors to dice it)
> 5 egg whites
> 5 tablespoons light brown sugar
> 2 cups skim milk
> 3 tablespoons nonfat dry milk
> 1 teaspoon vanilla extract

1.   Cut bread into ¾- to 1-inch chunks. Put them in a 12-by-7-inch glass or ceramic baking dish, together with the drained lychees, the mandarins and ½ cup of their juice, and the ginger.

2.   Beat the egg whites with 4 tablespoons of the sugar. Gently beat in the skim and dry milk and the vanilla. Pour the mixture over the bread. Use a broad spatula to push the bread into the liquid. Stir it gently, being careful not to break up the bread cubes. Sprinkle the additional tablespoon of sugar over the surface of the pudding. Cover the dish and refrigerate for several hours or overnight.

3.   Remove the dish from the refrigerator and let stand at room temperature while you preheat the oven to 350° F. Put the kettle on to boil.

4.   Choose a baking dish larger than the one with the bread and place it in the preheated oven. Put the smaller dish in the larger dish, and pour boiling water in the larger dish to come about halfway up the sides of the smaller one. Bake 30 to 40 minutes, until puffed and firm. (A knife inserted near the center will emerge clean.)

5.   Cool the bread pudding on a rack. Serve warm or at room temperature.

Peach Charlotte

S E R V E S   6

Per serving: 193.5 Cal. / 0 g fat / 0% fat / 0.92 mg cholesterol

Peach charlotte is a cross between French toast and bread pudding. Slices of custard-soaked bread are topped with fresh fruit and baked in a pie pan. Traditionally, French toast is made by soaking slices of stale bread in an eggy custard and then *frying* the slices in butter. Baking the soaked slices results in a much healthier (and more delicious) dish—a sort of custardy bread and fruit tart. To serve, cut in wedges like a pie.

1¼ cups diced peaches
¾ cup orange juice
¼ teaspoon almond extract
4 tablespoons light brown sugar
6 to 7 ounces thinly sliced stale bakery low-fat or nonfat white or whole wheat bread
3 egg whites
1 cup skim milk
2 tablespoons nonfat dry milk
1 teaspoon vanilla extract

1.   Combine the peaches, juice, almond extract, and 1 tablespoon sugar. Let soak for 15 to 30 minutes.
2.   Arrange the slices of bread so that they cover the bottom of an 11- to 12-inch nonstick pie pan. Cut the bread into halves and quarters if necessary.
3.   Pour the peaches and their juices evenly over the bread.
4.   Beat the egg whites with the remaining sugar. Gently beat in the remaining ingredients. Pour evenly over the bread and peaches. Cover and refrigerate for several hours or overnight.
5.   Preheat oven to 350° F. Bring bread and peaches to room temperature. Bake in a boiling water bath 35 to 45 minutes, until puffed and done (a knife inserted near the center will emerge clean). Serve at once, or cool on a rack.

Cinnamon-Almond French Toast

SERVES 4
Per serving: 268.1 Cal / 4.51 g fat / 15% fat / 207.5 mg cholesterol

Here we have slices of stale baguette soaked in cinnamon and almond-flavored custard and baked until the bread is creamy-textured within and crisp on top. Perfect for breakfast. Because this contains 3 whole eggs, it is not for those with high blood cholesterol levels.

> 6 ounces stale baguette, sliced ¾ inch thick
> 3 eggs
> 2 egg whites
> 3½ to 4 tablespoons superfine sugar
> 2 cups skim milk
> ½ teaspoon vanilla extract
> ½ teaspoon almond extract
> ½ teaspoon ground cinnamon

1. Arrange the slices of bread in overlapping rows so that they cover the bottom of a 12-by-7-inch glass or ceramic baking dish.
2. Beat the eggs and whites with the sugar. Gently beat in the remaining ingredients. Pour evenly over the bread. With a broad spatula, push the bread into the liquid. Cover and refrigerate for several hours or overnight.
3. Preheat oven to 350° F. Bring the bread mixture to room temperature. Bake in a boiling water bath 35 to 45 minutes, until puffed and done. Serve at once, or cool on a rack.

Rice Pudding

MAKES APPROXIMATELY 5 CUPS
Per ½ cup: 146.7 Cal. / 0.04 g fat / 0% fat / 2.53 mg cholesterol

This rice pudding is rich with the tastes and textures of caramelized milk and sugar, and creamy rice. The procedure
couldn't be simpler; stir the ingredients together (make sure
you use *short* grain rice—Italian Arborio works fine) and bake
in a hot water bath—that's all. You *do* have to stir it every
20 to 30 minutes, but that's not a difficult task, merely te-
dious. Tedium pays, however, and I'll wager that this is one
of the best rice puddings ever to soothe your soul.

> 6 tablespoons brown or golden raisins
> 6 tablespoons Amaretto di Saronno
> 3 tablespoons superfine sugar
> 5 cups skim milk, at room temperature
> 6 generous tablespoons nonfat dry milk
> 1 vanilla bean
> ½ cup plus 2 tablespoons short grain rice

1.   Combine the raisins and Amaretto in a small bowl and
let raisins soak while you preheat the oven to 300° F. Put the
kettle on to boil.
2.   Thoroughly stir together the sugar and skim and dry
milk. Split the vanilla bean lengthwise with a paring knife.
With the tip of the knife, scrape out the interior of the bean.
Add this black, aromatic material to the milk and stir thoroughly to mix it in. (Save the scraped bean for vanilla sugar
or granulated sugar substitute—see page 8.) Stir in the rice
and the raisins with their liqueur.
3.   Pour this mixture into a 9-inch square baking dish.
Choose another baking dish larger than the one with the rice

pudding and place it in the preheated oven. Put the smaller dish in the larger one, and pour boiling water into the larger dish so it comes two thirds of the way up the sides of the smaller one. Bake for approximately 2¼ hours, stirring every 20 to 30 minutes. It is done when the rice is tender and bathed in a thick, creamy sauce. It should not be *too* soupy, but on the other hand the liquid should not be completely absorbed. Serve warm or cold.

Creamy Yogurt Mousse

MAKES APPROXIMATELY 4 CUPS
Per cup: 146.6 Cal. / 0.01 g fat / 0% fat / 5.50 mg cholesterol

This recipe and the one that follows are for smooth milky mousses: the first of ginger and cardamom-scented yogurt, the second of vanilla-flavored farina. Comfort food—it's one of life's greatest pleasures.

> *2 cups skim milk*
> *½ cup nonfat dry milk*
> *2 cardamom pods, lightly crushed*
> *Pinch of ground ginger*
> *1½ envelopes plain gelatin*
> *½ cup cold water*
> *Pinch of salt*
> *½ cup sugar*
> *2 cups nonfat plain yogurt*

1.   Whisk together the skim and dry milk. Scald the milk with the cardamom pods and ginger in a heavy-bottomed saucepan. Meanwhile, soften the gelatin in the cold water.

2.   When the milk is scalded, add the salt and sugar and stir until dissolved. Stir in the softened gelatin. Cool to room temperature.

3.   Strain the mixture into a bowl. Lightly whisk the yogurt to smooth it out. (Don't overbeat or it will thin.) Stir the yogurt into the milk mixture and pour into a bowl or into individual dessert goblets. Chill several hours or overnight.

Farina Mousse

MAKES APPROXIMATELY 3 CUPS
Per ½ cup: 145.3 Cal. / 0 g fat / 0% fat / 2.50 mg cholesterol

¼ cup farina cereal
½ cup sugar
¼ cup nonfat dry milk
2 cups skim milk
½ teaspoon vanilla extract
1 cinnamon stick
1 envelope plain gelatin
¼ cup cold water
1 cup nonfat plain yogurt

1.   Combine the farina, sugar, dry and skim milk, vanilla, and cinnamon stick, and very slowly bring them to a boil in a heavy-bottomed pot, stirring constantly. Do not let the mixture scorch.

2.   Turn the heat to the lowest point and simmer about 5 minutes, stirring, until the mixture is thick, perfectly smooth, and cooked.

3. While the farina mixture is simmering, soften the gelatin in the cold water.

4. Stir the gelatin thoroughly into the farina mixture. Cool to room temperature.

5. Discard the cinnamon stick. Lightly whisk the yogurt to smooth it out. (Do not overbeat or it will thin.) Gently fold the yogurt into the farina mixture and pour into a glass bowl or into individual dessert goblets. Chill several hours or overnight.

Matzoh Carrot Pudding

SERVES 12

Per serving: 78.15 Cal. / 0.05 g fat / 1% fat / 0 mg cholesterol

This pudding is a recipe I've used for years. I "Slim Cuisined" it when I gave up fat. It is meant to be a sweet addition to the main course, rather than a dessert.

> *1 Granny Smith apple, peeled and grated*
> *2 tablespoons lemon juice*
> *½ cup sugar*
> *1¾ cups grated carrots (2½ medium-size carrots)*
> *¼ cup cream sherry or sweet dinner wine*
> *6 tablespoons medium matzoh meal (available all year in many supermarkets)*
> *6 egg whites, at room temperature*
> *Pinch of cream of tartar*
> *½ teaspoon cinnamon, or ½ teaspoon vanilla or almond extract*

1. Preheat oven to 375° F.
2. Toss together the grated apple, lemon juice, half the sugar, the grated carrots, the sherry, and the matzoh meal.
3. In an impeccably clean bowl, with an impeccably clean beater, beat the egg whites on medium speed until foamy. Add the cream of tartar and beat at higher speed until whites hold soft peaks. Beat in the remaining ¼ cup sugar, a little at a time, until it is dissolved and the egg whites hold firm peaks.
4. Stir two big spoonfuls of the egg whites into the carrot batter, to lighten it.
5. With a rubber spatula, fold the remaining egg whites into the carrot mixture. Sprinkle on the cinnamon or extract and fold it in. Pile the mixture into a 9-inch square baking dish. Bake until golden, and a thin skewer tests clean, about 35 minutes. Serve at once in squares.

Sweet Noodle Pudding

MAKES APPROXIMATELY 7 ½ CUPS
(This recipe can easily be halved or quartered.)
Per cup: 335.5 Cal. / 0.07 g fat / 0% fat / 0.11 mg cholesterol

In Eastern Europe, sweet noodle desserts are legion. I have had no luck in producing a decent Slim Cuisine version of a baked or fried noodle pudding, but boiled and tossed with a sweet and creamy sauce—that's another story. Boil up some broad noodles, dump them—hot and steaming—into fragrant vanilla- and orange-flavored cottage cheese, throw in a few plump raisins, and toss the whole together until each tender noodle is bathed in the aromatic sauce for a really blissful dish. This is not so much a dessert as a sweet main course, for those who love sweet things and are in need of some gastronomic coddling.

3 tablespoons brown raisins
3 tablespoons golden raisins
2 tablespoons water
2 tablespoons orange liqueur (Cointreau or Grand Marnier) (optional)
2 large oranges
1 large lemon
3½ cups nonfat cottage cheese or quark
2 tablespoons nonfat dry milk
1 teaspoon vanilla extract
3 tablespoons mild honey
1 pound broad noodles, such as tagliatelle
Light brown sugar to taste
Ground cinnamon

1. Combine the raisins, water, and orange liqueur in a small saucepan. Add the juice from both oranges and the slivered zest from one-half orange and one-half lemon. Simmer until the raisins are plump and the liquid has reduced to 1 to 2 tablespoons. Set aside.
2. Put the cheese, dry milk, vanilla, and honey in the food processor container. Zest the remaining halves of the orange and lemon right over the container, so that the zest as well as some of the aromatic oils go in. Process until very smooth and creamy. Set aside.
3. Warm a large bowl. Cook the noodles according to package directions. When they are tender but not mushy, drain well, then transfer to the warm bowl. With two large spoons, toss them with the raisins and their juices. Pour in the creamy mixture. Toss and turn with the two spoons until the noodles are thoroughly coated with the sauce.
4. Serve at *once* in deep, warm bowls. Provide a soup spoon

and fork for each diner. Have a shaker of cinnamon and a bowl of light brown sugar on the table. Each person can shake on cinnamon and sprinkle on sugar to taste.

ZESTING A CITRUS FRUIT

To zest a lemon, use a zester, which is an inexpensive little gadget that neatly removes fine slivers of zest from citrus fruit. If you wield the zester right over the bowl containing the rest of the recipe's ingredients, some of the aromatic oils will go in along with the slivers of zest. This is important: Zest lightly—the zest itself is lovely, but the white pith beneath it is strong and bitter. If you dig in too strenuously, the finished recipe may have an underlying bitter flavor. Another important point: Always scrub the citrus fruit before zesting, to remove any wax or traces of insecticide.

BE FRUITFUL

CAN SHE BAKE A CHERRY PIE?

Keeping in mind the French clafouti, a tender puffy, fruit-filled open pancake, I have worked out several low-fat versions of fruit flans. They may be prepared with no fat at all (except for a brief spritz of nonstick vegetable spray), or with just one egg yolk. And they may be prepared with white, oat, or whole wheat flour. Each, in its own way, is quite glorious. In preparing these flans, use a trusty, *nonstick* fluted pie pan, or, for the rectangular batter pudding versions, a glass or ceramic baking dish. Cool thoroughly before serving. To serve, use a triangular pie server. Cut a wedge or a square, then gently and carefully slide the pie server right under the wedge or square, separating it from the side and bottom of the dish. Carefully lift it up and put it on a plate. If you wish, pour some fruit coulis over each serving.

These flans deserve the best fresh fruit available. Use them to celebrate the bounty of the season.

Cherry-Peach Flan

SERVES 10   MAKES ONE 10-INCH FLAN
Per serving: 131.6 Cal. / 0.75 g fat / 5% fat / 0.70 mg cholesterol

This is wonderful. *No* egg yolks, therefore eliminating a big dose of fat. A tender pastry crust forms on the bottom, fluffy custard on top. See page 41 for the variations possible.

1 pound fresh peaches
1 pound sweet cherries
3 tablespoons light brown sugar
½ cup orange juice
2 teaspoons lemon juice
Grated zest of ½ lemon
Grated zest of ½ orange
Scant ¼ teaspoon almond extract
1 cup nonfat buttermilk
¼ cup nonfat dry milk
2 teaspoons vanilla extract
2 tablespoons granulated sugar
Pinch of salt
½ cup plus 3 tablespoons cake flour
½ teaspoon baking soda
5 egg whites

1. Preheat oven to 350° F.
2. Peel and pit the peaches and cut into wedges over a large measuring cup to catch their juices. Halve and pit the cherries over the cup. You want 4 cups of fruit in all. Combine the fruit with the brown sugar, juices, zest, and almond extract, and set aside.
3. Combine buttermilk, dry milk, vanilla extract, granulated sugar, salt, flour, baking soda, and egg whites in the blender jar. Process until very well blended.

4. Lightly coat an 11- to 12-inch nonstick pie pan with vegetable spray. Pour ½ to ¾ cup of the batter into the pan. Bake for 4 minutes. (Put a flat baking sheet on the bottom of the oven to catch any drips.) Top with the prepared fruit and juices. Pour the remaining batter over the fruit. Bake 50 to 60 minutes, until golden brown and puffed. Cool thoroughly on a rack. Serve at room temperature.

Apricot-Cherry Flan

SERVES 10   MAKES ONE 10-INCH FLAN
Per serving: 140.4 Cal. / 1.51 g fat / 10% fat / 28.10 mg cholesterol

Here is an equally wonderful (but quite different) one-yolk, oat flour version: In the finished flan, the fruit is surrounded by the tender dough.

1 pound fresh apricots
1 pound sweet cherries
3 tablespoons light brown sugar
½ cup orange juice
2 teaspoons lemon juice
Grated zest of ½ orange
Grated zest of ½ lemon
1 cup nonfat buttermilk
¼ cup nonfat dry milk
2 teaspoons vanilla extract
2 tablespoons granulated sugar
Pinch of salt
½ teaspoon baking soda
½ cup plus 3 tablespoons oat flour
3 egg whites
1 egg

1. Preheat oven to 350° F.
2. Peel the apricots and pit them over a measuring cup to catch the juices; cut into wedges. Halve and pit the cherries over the cup. You want 4 cups of fruit in all. Combine the fruit with the brown sugar, juices, and zest, and set aside.
3. Combine buttermilk, dry milk, vanilla extract, granulated sugar, salt, baking soda, oat flour, egg whites, and egg in the blender jar. Process until very well blended.
4. Lightly coat an 11-inch nonstick pie pan with vegetable spray. Pour ½ to ¾ cup of batter into the pan. Bake for 4 minutes. (Put a flat baking sheet on the bottom of the oven to catch any drips.) Top with the prepared fruit and juices. Pour the remaining batter over the fruit. Bake 50 to 60 minutes, until golden brown and puffed. Cool thoroughly on a rack. Serve at room temperature.

Apple-Raisin Flan

SERVES 10   MAKES ONE 10-INCH FLAN
Per serving: 122.3 Cal. / 0.71 g fat / 5% fat / 28.10 mg cholesterol

This is the white flour version of the one-yolk fruit flan; the dough has a bit more delicacy than the oat flour version.

1 pound Granny Smith apples, peeled, cored, and cut into wedges
3 tablespoons raisins
Slivered zest of ½ orange
Slivered zest of 1 lemon
½ cup orange juice
1 tablespoon lemon juice
3 tablespoons light brown sugar
1 cup nonfat buttermilk

¼ cup nonfat dry milk
2 teaspoons vanilla extract
2 tablespoons granulated sugar
Pinch of salt
½ teaspoon baking soda
½ cup plus 3 tablespoons cake flour
Pinch of ground cinnamon
Pinch of ground mace
Pinch of freshly grated nutmeg
3 egg whites
1 egg

1. Preheat oven to 350° F.
2. Combine the apples, raisins, and zest with the juice and brown sugar and set aside.
3. Combine buttermilk, dry milk, vanilla extract, granulated sugar, salt, baking soda, flour, cinnamon, mace, nutmeg, egg whites, and egg in the blender jar. Process until very well blended.
4. Lightly coat an 11-inch nonstick pie pan with vegetable spray. Pour ½ to ¾ cup of the batter into the pan. Bake for 4 minutes. (Put a flat baking sheet on the bottom of the oven to catch any drips.) Top with the prepared fruit and juices. Pour the remaining batter over the fruit. Bake for 50 to 60 minutes, until golden brown and puffed. Cool thoroughly on a rack. Serve at room temperature.

I I I I VARIATIONS I I I I

Pear-Raspberry Flan: Substitute 4 pears and 5 ounces raspberries for the apples and raisins.
Melon-Strawberry Flan: Substitute a mixture of 3 cups fruit.
Melon-Nectarine Flan: Substitute a mixture of 3 cups fruit.
Melon-Peach Flan: Substitute a mixture of 3 cups fruit.
Blueberry-Cherry Flan: Substitute a mixture of 3 cups fruit.

Blueberry Batter Pudding

SERVES 12

Per serving: 96.0 Cal. / 0.69 g fat / 6% fat / 23.42 mg cholesterol

This variation of the one-yolk, white flour clafouti batter, baked in a rectangular baking dish, makes a tender pudding-cake that is dense with juicy berries. To serve, cool *thoroughly* (it is best on the second day), cut into squares, carefully separate the bottom of the square from the dish with a triangular pie server, and lift out the square.

> 4½ cups (about 1 pound 6 ounces) blueberries, rinsed, drained, and picked over
> 5 tablespoons superfine sugar
> Slivered zest of ½ large orange
> ⅓ cup fresh orange juice
> Pinch of salt
> 3 egg whites
> 1 egg
> ¼ cup nonfat dry milk
> ½ cup nonfat buttermilk
> ½ cup plus 3 tablespoons oat flour
> ½ teaspoon baking soda

1. Preheat oven to 375° F.
2. Combine berries, 2 tablespoons sugar, orange zest and juice, and salt in a shallow 13½-by-8½-inch nonreactive baking dish (porcelain or pottery works best).
3. Combine all remaining ingredients, including the remaining 3 tablespoons sugar, in the container of a blender. Blend very well.
4. Pour batter evenly over the berries. Bake 40 to 50 minutes, until done. The blueberry juices will be bubbling up

through the batter and it may crack a bit, but that's fine. A skewer or toothpick will test clean. Cool *thoroughly* on a rack. (It's best on the following day.) Cut into squares and serve right from the pan.

Peach Batter Pudding

S E R V E S 1 2

Per serving: 87.33 Cal. / 0.71 g fat / 7% fat / 23.42 mg cholesterol

This is gorgeous—a *very* crumbly tender batter pudding with lots of peaches. Use the ripest, juiciest, most delicious peaches of summer for this one. To serve, cool thoroughly (it is best on the second day), cut in squares, and *gently* ease each square up with a pie server.

> *4 cups peeled, pitted, and diced ripe peaches,*
>   *including juices*
> *6 tablespoons superfine sugar*
> *½ teaspoon vanilla extract*
> *¾ teaspoon orange extract*
> *Slivered zest of ½ large orange*
> *⅓ cup fresh orange juice*
> *Pinch of salt*
> *3 egg whites*
> *1 egg*
> *¼ cup nonfat dry milk*
> *1 cup nonfat buttermilk*
> *½ cup plus 3 tablespoons oat flour*
> *½ teaspoon baking soda*

1. Preheat oven to 375° F.
2. Combine peaches, their juices, 3 tablespoons sugar, va-

nilla and orange extracts, orange zest, and orange juice in a shallow, rectangular ovenproof 13½-by-8½-inch baking dish.
3. Combine all remaining ingredients, including the remaining 3 tablespoons sugar, in the container of the blender. Blend very well.
4. Pour batter evenly over the peaches. Bake 35 to 40 minutes, until done. (It will be puffed and browned, and a skewer of toothpick will test clean.) Cool thoroughly on a rack. Cut into squares and serve right from the pan.

Red and Blue Fruit Batter Pudding

SERVES 12
Per serving: 112.8 Cal. / 1.24 g fat / 10% fat / 23.42 mg cholesterol

This version of the rectangular clafouti one-yolk batter pudding has three sections: red (cherries), blue (blueberries), and red again (raspberries). Cut and serve as described in the previous recipes.

10 ounces pitted, halved sweet cherries
10 ounces raspberries
10 ounces blueberries
6 tablespoons superfine sugar
⅓ cup orange juice
½ teaspoon vanilla extract
Pinch of salt
3 egg whites
1 egg
¼ cup nonfat dry milk
1 cup nonfat buttermilk
½ teaspoon baking soda
½ cup plus 3 tablespoons oat flour
½ teaspoon baking soda

1. Preheat oven to 375° F.
2. Toss together the fruit, 3 tablespoons of the sugar, the orange juice, vanilla, and salt. Put mixture in a 10-inch square glass or ceramic baking dish.
3. Combine all remaining ingredients, including the remaining 3 tablespoons sugar, in the container of the blender. Blend well.
4. Pour the batter evenly over the fruit. Bake 40 to 50 minutes, until done. It will be puffed and browned, and a skewer or toothpick will test clean. Cool thoroughly on a rack. (It's best on the following day.) Cut into squares and serve right from the pan.

No-Sugar, No-Cook Summer Pudding ♡

SERVES 4

Per serving: 251.3 Cal. / 1.49 g fat / 5% fat / 0 mg cholesterol

This is a no-added-sugar version of a delightful English dish. Who would have guessed that you could take some old bread, some ripe berries, a pudding basin (it sounds exotic, but it's just a plain old bowl), and put them together in such a glorious way?

> 7 to 8 thin slices low-fat or nonfat bakery white bread, one
> to two days old
> 1¾ pounds mixed red fruit: halved strawberries, whole
> raspberries, and pitted and halved or quartered red cherries
> Granulated sugar substitute to taste
> ½ pound strawberries

1. Trim the crusts from the bread and cut trimmed slices diagonally into quarters. Use some of them to line the bottom

and sides of a 5-cup glass bowl. Cut or tear small pieces of bread to patch any spaces.

2. Put the mixed red fruits in a bowl, and crush with a potato masher until the juices run. Sweeten to taste, and crush and mash a bit more. Pour the fruit and juices into the bread-lined bowl. Use the remaining bread pieces to cover the fruit, leaving no spaces. Choose a saucer or plate that fits in the bowl, and place it on top of the pudding. Put a can on the plate to weight it. If possible remove a shelf from the refrigerator so there is plenty of head room. Put the pudding in the refrigerator, place a cutting board over the can on the saucer, and put two more big cans on the board. Leave for at *least* 8 hours.

3. Remove the weights and plate. Loosen the sides of the pudding with a palette knife. Turn out onto a plate.

4. Hull and halve the remaining ½ pound of strawberries. In a bowl, mash and crush them with a potato masher until the juices run. Sweeten to taste with granulated sugar substitute. Use this sauce to paint any mottled patches on the pudding. Surround the pudding with the remaining sauce and cut into wedges to serve.

Winter Pudding

SERVES 6

Per serving: 347.7 Cal. / 0 g fat / 0% fat / 0 mg cholesterol

When berries are out of season, and you don't have any frozen ones handy, try substituting a compote of diced, dried fruits for the red fruit in the summer pudding recipe. *Luscious* is the word that comes to mind. The bread soaks up the syrupy compote juices: The contrasting textures of the juice-soaked bread and the fruit pieces, coupled with the sweet-tart balance of flavors, make this pudding outstanding.

DRIED FRUIT COMPOTE
¼ cup golden raisins
3 cups (1 pound) dried fruit (apricots, apples, figs, prunes, pears), diced
1 cup water
1 cup dry white wine or apple cider
¼ cup sugar
½ cinnamon stick
Juice and grated zest of 1 lemon
½ to ¾ cup fresh orange juice

7 to 8 thin slices low-fat or nonfat bakery white bread, one to two days old

1. Combine the golden raisins, mixed dried fruit, water, and the wine or cider in a baking dish. Allow to soak for 1 hour.
2. Preheat the oven to 350° F.
3. At the end of the hour, stir in the sugar, cinnamon stick, and lemon juice and zest. Cover the dish and bake for 1 hour. Cool and refrigerate until needed (it keeps for weeks).
4. When the compote has thoroughly cooled, remove the cinnamon stick and stir in ½ to ¾ cup fresh orange juice.
5. Line a 5-cup glass bowl with bread as for No-Sugar, No-Cook Summer Pudding (page 45), and fill with the fruit compote. Cover the fruit with bread and weight as in previous recipe. Refrigerate for at *least* 8 hours.
6. When you turn the pudding out onto a plate, paint any pale bits with orange juice.

Fruit Soufflé

S E R V E S   3   O R   4

Per serving (⅓): 106.2 Cal. / 0 g fat / 0% fat / 0 mg cholesterol
(¼): 79.65 Cal. / 0 g fat / 0% fat / 0 mg cholesterol

In the dead of winter, pull out a can of fruit, whip up a few egg whites, and in 15 minutes you have a gossamer, fruit-imbued soufflé that almost floats out of its dish.

> One 14- to 15-ounce can fruit in natural juice (pears, apricots, or peaches)
> 1 tablespoon orange liqueur (Cointreau or Grand Marnier) (optional)
> 3 egg whites, at room temperature
> Pinch of salt
> Pinch of cream of tartar
> 1 to 2 tablespoons sugar

1.   Preheat oven to 400° F.
2.   Drain fruit and mash with a potato masher to a rough purée. Stir in the liqueur.
3.   Beat egg whites in an electric mixer on medium speed until foamy. Add salt and cream of tartar and beat on highest speed, adding sugar a little at a time, until the sugar is dissolved and the whites are shiny and thick and hold firm peaks.
4.   Stir a tablespoon of the meringue into the fruit purée to lighten it. Fold in the remainder. Spoon the mixture into a 5-cup soufflé dish. Bake 15 to 20 minutes, or until beautifully puffed and golden. Serve at once.

Banana Soufflé

S E R V E S   4   T O   6

Per serving (¼): 144.7 Cal. / 0.11 g fat / 1% fat / 0 mg cholesterol
          (⅙): 96.46 Cal. / 0.08 g fat / 1% fat / 0 mg cholesterol

This soufflé and the one that follows (as with the previous canned fruit version) contain none of the usually traditional egg yolks—just the whites, plenty of fruit, a bit of sugar, and some flavoring. They are dramatic creations, and very, very simple to make.

> *3 medium-size ripe bananas*
> *1 tablespoon dark rum*
> *¼ teaspoon grated nutmeg*
> *½ teaspoon cinnamon*
> *1 scant tablespoon lemon juice*
> *8 egg whites, at room temperature*
> *Pinch of cream of tartar*
> *Approximately 2 tablespoons sugar (less if the bananas are*
> *   very sweet)*
> *½ teaspoon vanilla*

1.   Preheat the oven to 350° F. Remove one oven shelf and position remaining shelf in the middle of the oven.
2.   Cut bananas into thick slices. Purée with the rum, the spices, and the lemon juice in a food processor or blender. Scrape into a large bowl.
3.   Beat egg whites in an electric mixer on medium speed until foamy. Add cream of tartar and beat on highest speed, adding sugar a little at a time, until the sugar is dissolved and the whites are shiny and thick and hold firm peaks. Fold in the vanilla.
4.   Gently fold the whites into the banana mixture.

||||||||||||||||||||||||||||||||||||||||||||||||||||||||||||||||||||||||||||||||

5. Spoon banana mixture into an 8- to 9-cup soufflé dish. Bake 30 to 35 minutes. Serve at once.

NOTE: If you wish to gild the lily, serve with Hot Chocolate Sauce (page 121) or Raspberry Coulis (page 124).

Mango Soufflé

S E R V E S 4 T O 6

Per serving (¼): 195.1 Cal. / 0 g fat / 0% fat / 0 mg cholesterol
      (⅙): 130.1 Cal. / 0 g fat / 0% fat / 0 mg cholesterol

   3 large ripe mangoes, peeled, pitted, and diced
   1½ teaspoons lime juice
   2 tablespoons cornstarch
   ¼ cup water
   3 tablespoons dark rum
   2 tablespoons sugar
   8 egg whites, at room temperature

1. Preheat the oven to 350° F. Remove one oven shelf and position the other in the middle of the oven.
2. Purée mangoes and lime juice in the food processor.
3. Combine cornstarch and water and whisk until a smooth paste forms.
4. Stir cornstarch mixture into the mango purée. In a saucepan, bring to the boil, reduce heat, and simmer for 4 or 5 minutes, until very thick.
5. Stir in rum and 1 tablespoon sugar and cook for 1 minute more. Scrape into a large bowl and leave to cool.
6. Beat egg whites in an electric mixer on medium speed until foamy. Add remaining sugar, a little at a time, while beating on highest speed, until the sugar is dissolved and the whites are shiny and thick and hold firm peaks.
7. Gently fold the whites into the mango mixture.

8. Spoon the mango mixture into an 8- to 9-cup soufflé dish. Bake 35 to 40 minutes. Serve at once.

Pear–Sweet Potato Meringue

SERVES 10 TO 12

Per serving ($\frac{1}{10}$): 113.4 Cal. / 0.40 g fat / 3% fat / 0 mg cholesterol
($\frac{1}{12}$): 94.48 Cal. / 0.33 g fat / 3% fat / 0 mg cholesterol

Here is a new healthy version of grandma's "candied yams." It's made from sweet potatoes and pears—a marriage made in heaven. Layer them in a gratin dish, brush with honey and orange juice, dust with cinnamon, and bake under a blanket of apricot and vanilla scented meringue. This is comfort food at its finest. This recipe is meant to be a sweet accompaniment to a holiday dinner rather than merely a dessert

> 4 pears, peeled and thinly sliced
> 2 sweet potatoes (approximately ½ pound each), peeled and
>   thinly sliced
> 1½ tablespoons mild honey
> ½ to ¾ cup orange juice
> 2 teaspoons water
> Pinch or two of ground cinnamon

TOPPING

> 2 egg whites at room temperature
> Pinch of cream of tartar
> 1 to 1½ tablespoons sugar
> 2 teaspoons orange liqueur (optional)
> 1 teaspoon vanilla extract
> 1 tablespoon no-sugar apricot fruit spread

1. Preheat oven to 400° F.
2. Overlap alternating thin slices of pear and sweet potato in a 12-by-7½-inch gratin dish.
3. Stir together 1 tablespoon honey and the orange juice and pour over the pears and potatoes.
4. In a small bowl, mix together the remaining ½ tablespoon honey with the water and cinnamon and use it to brush over the pears and potatoes as they bake.
5. Bake approximately 45 minutes to 1 hour, until tender but not mushy, and caramelized.
6. With an electric mixer, beat the egg whites until they are foamy. Add a pinch of cream of tartar and beat until they hold firm peaks, gradually adding the sugar, orange liqueur, vanilla extract, and apricot fruit spread as you beat.
7. Spread the meringue topping over the pear–sweet potato base and bake for a further 10 minutes until golden. Serve hot or warm.

Apple-Raisin Meringue

SERVES 10

Per serving: 56.57 Cal. / 0.01 g fat / 0% fat / 0 mg cholesterol

An apple-raisin version of the preceding pear–sweet potato meringue. I leave the apples unpeeled, because I like the leathery texture of the baked apple skins, but you may peel them if you prefer.

4 tart eating apples, sliced
¼ cup raisins
1 tablespoon plus ½ teaspoon honey
½ cup orange juice

Slivered zest of 1 lemon
2 pinches of ground cinnamon
1 pinch of freshly grated nutmeg
2 teaspoons water

TOPPING

2 egg whites, at room temperature
Pinch of cream of tartar
1 to 1½ tablespoons sugar
2 teaspoons calvados, brandy, or dark rum (optional)
1 teaspoon vanilla extract
1 tablespoon no-sugar apricot fruit spread

1. Preheat oven to 400° F.
2. Overlap the slices of apple in a 12-by-7½-inch glass gratin dish. Sprinkle the raisins over the apples.
3. Mix together 1 tablespoon honey, the orange juice, lemon zest, cinnamon, and nutmeg and pour over the apples and raisins.
4. In a small bowl, combine the remaining ½ teaspoon honey and the water and use to brush over the apples and raisins as they bake.
5. Bake 15 to 20 minutes, until the apples are *just* tender, not mushy. Flash under the broiler to caramelize a bit if necessary.
6. With an electric mixer, beat the egg whites until they are foamy. Add a pinch of cream of tartar and beat until they hold firm peaks, adding the sugar, calvados, vanilla extract, and apricot fruit spread as you beat.
7. Spread the meringue topping over the apples and bake for a further 10 minutes until golden. Serve hot or warm.

Banana Roulade   ✳

S E R V E S   1 2

Per serving: 70.17 Cal. / 0.08 g fat / 1% fat / 0 mg cholesterol

To make a banana roulade, an airy soufflélike banana–egg
white batter is baked flat, cooled, filled with Chocolate "Butter" (page 163), Fig Butter (page 95), or Chestnut-Chocolate
Cream (page 170) and rolled.

> *3 very ripe bananas*
> *1 tablespoon thawed orange juice concentrate*
> *½ teaspoon freshly grated nutmeg*
> *½ teaspoon ground cinnamon*
> *1 scant tablespoon lemon juice*
> *8 egg whites, at room temperature*
> *Pinch of cream of tartar*
> *Approximately 2 tablespoons sugar (less if the bananas are
>   very sweet)*
> *½ teaspoon vanilla extract*
> *½ cup plus 1 tablespoon cake flour, sifted*
> *Confectioners' sugar*

1.   Line a nonstick 13-by-9-inch baking sheet with baking
parchment. Set aside.
2.   Preheat oven to 350° F.
3.   Cut bananas into thick slices. Purée with the orange juice
concentrate, the spices, and the lemon juice in a food processor or blender. Scrape into a large bowl.
4.   Beat egg whites in an electric mixer on medium speed
until foamy. Add cream of tartar and beat on highest speed,
adding sugar a little at a time, until the sugar is dissolved and
the whites are shiny and thick and hold firm peaks. Fold in
the vanilla.

5. Gently fold the whites into the banana mixture, together with the sifted flour.

6. Gently spoon and spread all the banana mixture onto the prepared baking sheet. Smooth the top with the back of your spoon. It will seem like an enormous amount of batter, but don't worry. After it bakes and cools, it collapses somewhat. Bake 20 to 25 minutes; when done, the surface will spring back when lightly pressed, and a toothpick will test clean. Cool in the pan on a rack.

7. Spread a clean dish towel on your work surface. Cover with a sheet of wax or greaseproof paper. Sprinkle lightly and evenly with confectioners' sugar. When it is thoroughly cooled, turn the roulade base out onto the paper, then peel off the parchment.

8. Spread the base with the filling of your choice. Starting with a long edge, roll the base like a jelly roll, using the dish towel to help you roll. It may crack a bit, but it doesn't matter. Chill until needed. Serve in slices.

Grilled Bananas and Rum ◷

S E R V E S   3   O R   4

Per serving (¼): 107.9 Cal. / 0 g fat / 0% fat / 0 mg cholesterol

Versions of bananas sautéed in butter and flamed in rum occur in several cuisines. This version *bakes* them in orange juice and a touch of rum and brown sugar, with the same delectably rich result. To shock and delight the senses, try serving each portion of the bananas piping hot with a scoop of cold creamy Banana–Ginger Sorbet (page 136) on top.

3 very ripe bananas
Juice of ½ lime
Juice of ½ lemon
¼ to ½ cup fresh orange juice
1 tablespoon dark rum
1 heaped tablespoon light brown sugar

1.   Preheat broiler to its highest setting.
2.   Peel the bananas, cut in half lengthwise, then cut each half in half crosswise.
3.   Put the citrus juices and rum in a shallow baking dish that can hold the banana pieces in one layer. Turn the bananas in the juice. Arrange, cut sides down, in one layer, and sprinkle evenly with brown sugar.
4.   Broil 3 inches from the heat for 3 to 5 minutes, or until the bananas are well browned on top.
5.   Tilt the dish and drain the juices into a small saucepan or frying pan. Boil the juices briefly to thicken them.
6.   Pour the juices back over the bananas. Top each hot serving with a dollop of Honeyed Vanilla Cream (page 99) or Banana-Ginger Sorbet (see recipe).

IIII VARIATION IIII

♡   Omit sugar. Serve with Banana-Ginger Sorbet.
Per serving (1/4): 95.9 Cal. / 0 g fat / 0% fat / 0 mg cholesterol

Broiled Bananas in Their Jackets ♡ ⊕

Per banana: 105.0 Cal. / 0 g fat / 0% fat / 0 mg cholesterol

Broiling a banana (or grilling it on a charcoal grill) intensifies its natural sweetness and turns it into a banana custard within its skin. This has to be one of the easiest (and sweetest!) of desserts.

Preheat the broiler. Line the broiler tray with foil, shiny side up. Place the rack on the broiler tray. Choose very ripe bananas and put these—unpeeled—on the broiler rack. Broil about 1 inch from the heat for approximately 3 minutes on each side, until the bananas have swelled up, are speckled with charred bits, and are spitting and spluttering like mad. With tongs, carefully transfer the bananas to a plate. Peel a strip off the top of each. Pour any juices from the broiler tray onto the bananas. Eat with a spoon.

Stuffed Peaches

MAKES 12 HALVES
Per serving: 41.42 Cal. / 0 g fat / 0% fat / 0 mg cholesterol

This is a low-fat, low-sugar version of a very elegant Italian dessert. Save it for summer, when the peaches are ripe, juicy, and bursting with flavor.

> 7 ripe, firm peaches
> 3 pairs amaretti cookies
> ¼ teaspoon vanilla extract
> 6 tablespoons orange liqueur (Cointreau or Grand Marnier)
> ¾ cup medium sweet marsala or sherry

1. Preheat the oven to 375° F.
2. Carefully halve the peaches. (Work over the bowl to catch any juices.) Remove the pits, trim any bits of peach flesh off them, and add to the juices. Chop up two of the peach halves

and put in the bowl with the juices. Using a teaspoon, slightly hollow out the depressions in the remaining peach halves, so that they will hold the filling. Add the peach pulp that you have scooped out to the bowl. Place the peaches, skin side down, in a baking dish that holds them snugly in one layer.
3.   Crumble the amaretti and stir them into the peach juices and chopped peach bits. Stir in the vanilla and ½ teaspoon of orange liqueur. Combine the remaining liqueur with the marsala or sherry.
4.   Fill each peach half with an equal amount of the amaretti mixture. Pour ½ to ¾ cup of the marsala mixture around the peaches. Sprinkle them with another 2 to 3 tablespoons of the mixture.
5.   Bake, uncovered, 10 to 12 minutes. Sprinkle stuffed peaches evenly with another 3 to 4 tablespoons of the marsala mixture and bake for 8 to 10 minutes more. The peaches should not lose their shape.
6.   With a slotted spoon, remove the peaches to a pretty serving dish. Serve the peaches warm or at room temperature, on a pool of the boiled-down cooking juices.

Pears Filled with Orange Cream   ♡

MAKES 8 HALVES

Per serving: 133.9 Cal. / 2.40 g fat / 16% fat / 7.00 mg cholesterol

The orange cream that fills these pears is simply low-fat ricotta flavored with orange juice concentrate, vanilla, and a bit of sweetener. The pears should be well chosen—juicy and sweet (canned pears won't do here!). The crunchy topping is provided by Grape-Nuts (crush the cereal in a plastic bag with a rolling pin, or briefly whirl it in the blender), and Raspberry Coulis provides a touch of color and intensity of flavor.

14 ounces low-fat ricotta cheese
Granulated sugar substitute to taste
3 tablespoons thawed orange juice concentrate
1 teaspoon vanilla extract
Pinch of grated nutmeg
4 large pears
Juice of 1 lemon
Grape-Nuts
Raspberry Coulis (page 124)

1. In a food processor, blend the ricotta, sweetener, orange juice concentrate, vanilla, and nutmeg. Set aside.
2. Peel and halve the pears and remove the cores with a small spoon, forming a cavity. Roll the pears thoroughly in lemon juice.
3. Stuff the pear cavities with the ricotta mixture and carefully spread the cut sides of the pears with the mixture. Sprinkle the cereal over the "cream"-filled pears so they are evenly coated. Cover with plastic wrap and refrigerate until needed.
4. Place each pear half on a plate. Pour the Raspberry Coulis around the pears.

HAVE YOUR CAKE

Angel Cake

Making a cake without a speck of fat and oil is easy. In fact, one of the most classic cakes of all, the angel cake, is made exactly that way—no egg yolks, no butter, no oil, no shortening of any sort, not even a smear to grease the pan. A successful angel cake is tender and airy, and fun to make.

The rules for making angel cake are similar to the rules for making soufflés:

1. You will need to separate the yolks and whites of several eggs. Cold eggs separate easier than room temperature ones, but room temperature egg whites whip up to a greater volume than chilled ones. As a result it's best to separate the yolks from the whites while the eggs are cold, then allow the whites to reach room temperature before whipping them.

2. Always make sure that every speck of yolk is gone from the white, and that your bowl and beater are impeccably clean. Even a speck of grease will inhibit the whites from whipping into a cloud of meringue.
3. A pinch of cream of tartar adds a bit of acidity and enables the egg whites to whip to their maximum volume.

A FEW WORDS ABOUT ANGEL CAKE PANS

A classic angel cake should be made in an angel cake pan, which is a tube pan with a removable bottom inside the pan. Angel cakes should be cooled upside down. To do this, carefully invert the pan over a bottle or inverted funnel. The neck of the bottle or funnel should come right through the tube. After the cake has cooled—at least an hour, preferably more—loosen it around the sides with a long flexible spatula. Let the cake slide out onto a serving plate, then loosen the tube bottom piece with a spatula and lift the bottom off. The cake is served upside down.

Angel Cake

SERVES 12   MAKES ONE 10-INCH CAKE
Per serving: 119.9 Cal. / 0.07 g fat / 1% fat / 0 mg cholesterol

1 cup cake flour
1¼ cups plus 1 tablespoon superfine sugar
10 egg whites, at room temperature
Pinch of cream of tartar
1½ teaspoons vanilla extract

1. Preheat the oven to 375° F.
2. Sift together the flour and ½ cup sugar.
3. Beat the egg whites until foamy. Add the cream of tartar and beat until they hold soft peaks. Continue beating, adding the remaining sugar, 2 tablespoons at a time, until the sugar is dissolved and the whites are stiff and glossy. Fold in the vanilla.
4. A little at a time, sprinkle the sifted flour/sugar mixture over the batter and fold in gently but thoroughly.
5. Gently spoon and push the meringue into an ungreased 10-inch angel cake pan 4 to 4½ inches deep. Bake 35 to 40 minutes. When the cake is done the top will probably have cracked like a soufflé. The cake will spring back when gently pressed with your finger, and a cake tester will test clean.
6. Cool *upside down* by inverting the cake—in its pan—on a bottle (the neck of the bottle should come right up through the hole), or on an inverted funnel. Leave for at least 1 hour.
7. Use a long palette knife to loosen the cake gently along the sides of the pan, and around the tube. Gently shake, and slide out onto a plate. Use a flexible spatula to loosen the cake from the pan bottom and lift out the tube. To serve, cut gently, using a sawing motion, with a long, sharp, serrated knife.

‖‖

IIII VARIATION IIII

MAKES ONE 10-INCH CAKE

Per serving: 128.8 Cal. / 0.39 g fat / 3% fat / 0 mg cholesterol

Chocolate Angel Cake: Reduce the amount of flour to ¾ cup plus 1 tablespoon. In Step 2, sift in 6 tablespoons cocoa.

Black and White Angel Cake

SERVES 12   MAKES ONE 10-INCH CAKE

Per serving: 119.6 Cal. / 0.22 g fat / 2% fat / 0 mg cholesterol

The best of both worlds—an angel cake that is half vanilla and half chocolate.

Slices of angel cake are absolutely splendid when toasted. Top the toasted cake with Fruit Compote (page 96), a scoop of Slim Cuisine Food Processor Ice Creams (page 120), Hot Chocolate Sauce (page 121), fresh berries, or whatever pleases you.

> *¾ cup cake flour*
> *1⅓ cups superfine sugar*
> *3 tablespoons cocoa powder*
> *10 egg whites, at room temperature*
> *Pinch of cream of tartar*
> *1½ teaspoons vanilla extract*

1. Preheat oven to 375° F.
2. Sift together ½ cup cake flour and ¼ cup superfine sugar. Set aside.

3. Sift together ¼ cup cake flour, 3 tablespoons cocoa powder, and ⅓ cup superfine sugar. Set aside.

4. Beat the egg whites with the cream of tartar until they hold soft peaks. Beat in ¾ cup superfine sugar, 2 tablespoons at a time, until the sugar is dissolved and the whites are stiff and glossy and hold firm peaks. Fold in the vanilla.

5. Divide the mixture in half. Into one half fold in the white flour/sugar mixture, into the other half, fold in the cocoa/flour mixture.

6. Gently spoon and push the white batter into the ungreased angel cake pan. Spoon and push the chocolate batter evenly over the white. Bake 30 to 35 minutes. (The cake is done when it springs back when gently poked with your finger, and a cake tester tests clean.)

7. Cool *upside down* by inverting the pan on a bottle (the neck of the bottle should come right up through the hole), or on an inverted funnel. Leave for at *least* 1 hour.

8. Use a long palette knife to gently loosen the cake along the sides of the pan, and around the tube. Gently shake, and slide out onto a plate. Use the flexible spatula to loosen the cake from the pan bottom, and lift out the tube. To serve, cut gently, using a sawing motion, with a long, sharp, serrated knife.

Angel Sheet Cake

S E R V E S   1 0

Per serving: 135.4 Cal. / 0.08 g fat / 1% fat / 0 mg cholesterol

Angel cake batters baked flat to make a sheet cake can be cut and filled to make layer cakes (see variation).

1 cup cake flour
1 cup plus 2 tablespoons superfine sugar
10 egg whites, at room temperature
Pinch of cream of tartar
2 teaspoons vanilla extract

1. Preheat the oven to 350° F.
2. Sift together the flour and ½ cup sugar. Set aside.
3. Beat the egg whites until foamy. Add the cream of tartar and beat until they hold soft peaks. Continue beating, adding the remaining sugar, 2 tablespoons at a time, until the sugar is dissolved, and the whites are stiff and glossy. Fold in the vanilla.
4. A little at a time, sprinkle the sifted flour/sugar mixture over the batter and fold in gently but thoroughly.
5. Spread the mixture onto a 13-by-9-inch baking sheet lined with baking parchment.
6. Bake for 15 to 18 minutes.
7. Allow to cool in the pan on a rack. Spread a dish towel on your work surface, invert the cooled cake onto it, and carefully peel off the paper.

▌▌▌▌ VARIATION ▌▌▌▌

Layer Cake: Bake the Angel Sheet Cake according to the instructions above. After removing the parchment, cut the cake into thirds. Spread each piece with Chocolate "Butter" (page 163) and stack. Ice the top and sides with Chocolate "Butter."

Chocolate Angel Sheet Cake

S E R V E S   10   T O   12

Per serving (¹/₁₀): 140.4 Cal. / 0.47 g fat / 3% fat / 0 mg cholesterol
(¹/₁₂): 117.0 Cal. / 0.39 g fat / 3% fat / 0 mg cholesterol

¾ cup plus ½ tablespoon cake flour
6 tablespoons cocoa powder
1 cup plus 2 tablespoons superfine sugar
10 egg whites, at room temperature
Pinch of cream of tartar
2 teaspoons vanilla extract

1. Preheat the oven to 350° F.
2. Sift together the flour, cocoa, and ½ cup sugar. Set aside.
3. Beat the egg whites until foamy. Add the cream of tartar and beat until they hold soft peaks. Continue beating, adding the remaining sugar, 2 tablespoons at a time, until the sugar is dissolved and the whites are stiff and glossy. Fold in the vanilla.
4. A little at a time, sprinkle the sifted mixture over the batter and fold in gently but thoroughly.
5. Spread the mixture onto a 13-by-9-inch baking sheet lined with baking parchment.
6. Bake for 15 to 18 minutes.
7. Allow to cool on a rack. Spread a dish towel on your work surface, turn the cooled cake out onto it, and carefully peel off the paper.

▌▌▌▌ VARIATION ▌▌▌▌

Per serving: 178.3 Cal. / 0.44 g fat / 2% fat / 0.41 mg cholesterol
Chocolate Layer Cake: Bake the Chocolate Angel Sheet Cake according to the instructions above. After removing the

parchment paper, cut the cake into thirds. Spread layers with either Chocolate "Butter" (page 163), Mocha "Butter" (page 164), or one of the ricotta mixtures used in the Tiramisù recipes (pages 152–55). Ice top and sides with either of the "butters."

Stir-Crazy Chocolate Cake ⏳

SERVES 12   MAKES ONE 11-INCH CAKE
Per serving: 111.8 Cal. / 0.44 g fat / 4% fat / 0.33 mg cholesterol

The Stir Crazy (sometimes called crazy cake or wacky cake) is an old recipe. Rumor has it that it originated in the American Southwest, as part of the chuckwagon cuisine of the American cowboy, but I believe its true source was an ingenious mother faced with the pressing need for a large, child-pleasing dessert that had to be rapidly prepared with basic pantry ingredients.

Why not serve wedges of Stir Crazy topped with scoops of Chocolate Sorbet (page 118) or Milk Chocolate Ice Cream (page 110)? Why not add a pool of Strawberry or Raspberry Coulis (page 124)? And how about a scattering of fresh raspberries in season?

1¼ cups unbleached all-purpose flour
½ teaspoon baking soda
¾ cup plus 2 tablespoons superfine sugar
⅓ cup cocoa powder
Pinch of salt
1 teaspoon vanilla extract
1 cup nonfat buttermilk
½ cup water

1. Preheat oven to 350° F.
2. Sift the flour, baking soda, sugar, cocoa, and salt directly into a 12-inch nonstick quiche or flan dish. Combine the vanilla, buttermilk, and water and pour the mixture over the dry ingredients in the pan.
3. With a wooden spoon, stir the mixture together in the pan, using a gentle circular motion, until the dry ingredients are thoroughly incorporated into the liquid ones.
4. Bake for approximately 15 minutes, until *just* done. The surface will spring back when lightly pressed and a cake tester will test clean. Cool on a rack. Serve in wedges right from the pan.

I I I I   VARIATION   I I I I

To make a stir-crazy layer cake, double the Stir-Crazy Chocolate Cake recipe to make two layers, and fill them with Chestnut-Chocolate Cream (page 170). If you wish, ice the top and sides with Chocolate "Butter" (page 163).

Stir-Crazy Banana-Fudge Cake ⊕

SERVES 12   MAKES ONE 11-INCH CAKE
Per serving: 110.7 Cal. / 0.42 g fat / 3% fat / 0.17 mg cholesterol

The addition of mashed ripe banana to the basic stir crazy turned out to be a very good idea. It can be served with a scoop of Banana Ice Cream (page 114). Or how about a scoop of Banana Ice Cream and a nice puddle of Hot Chocolate Sauce (page 121)?

1¼ cups unbleached all-purpose flour
½ teaspoon baking soda
½ cup plus 2 tablespoons superfine sugar
⅓ cup cocoa powder
Pinch of salt
1 teaspoon vanilla extract
½ cup nonfat buttermilk
½ cup water
2 very ripe bananas, peeled and mashed to a pulp

1.   Preheat the oven to 350° F.
2.   Sift the flour, baking soda, sugar, cocoa, and salt directly into a 12-inch nonstick quiche or flan dish. Combine the vanilla, buttermilk, and water and pour the mixture over the dry ingredients in the pan. Add banana pulp.
3.   With a wooden spoon, stir the mixture together right in the pan, using a gentle, circular motion, until the dry ingredients are thoroughly incorporated into the liquid ones. The mixture may be a little lumpy from the banana pulp, but that's fine.
4.   Bake for approximately 15 to 20 minutes, until *just* done; the surface will spring back when lightly pressed, and a cake tester will test clean.
5.   Cool on a rack. Serve in wedges right from the pan.

Stir-Crazy Chocolate-Raspberry Cake

S E R V E S   1 2
Per serving: 139.6 Cal. / 0.77 g fat / 5% fat / 0.33 mg cholesterol

The stir–crazy batter can be mixed in a bowl and then poured into a rectangular baking dish. Scatter on some fresh raspberries, bake, and cool. The result is very like a raspberry brownie.

1¼ cups unbleached all-purpose flour
½ teaspoon baking soda
¾ cup plus 2 tablespoons superfine sugar
⅓ cup cocoa powder
Pinch of salt
1 teaspoon vanilla extract
½ cup water
1 cup nonfat buttermilk
4 cups fresh raspberries
2 tablespoons granulated sugar

1. Preheat oven to 350° F.
2. Sift together the flour, baking soda, superfine sugar, cocoa, and salt into a bowl. In a 2-cup measure, combine the vanilla, water, and buttermilk. Pour the liquid mixture over the dry ingredients in the bowl. With a wooden spoon, stir the mixture together using a gentle circular motion until the dry ingredients are thoroughly incorporated into the liquid ones.
3. Pour and scrape the batter into a 13½-by-8½-inch oven-proof baking dish 2 inches deep. With a rubber spatula, spread it evenly over the dish.
4. Combine the raspberries and sugar (be careful not to crush or break up the raspberries) and pour and scatter the mixture in one even layer over the chocolate batter, leaving a ½-inch border all around.
5. Bake for approximately 50 minutes. The edges of the cake will be set, and the surface, when pressed around the edges, will spring back. The raspberry center will remain somewhat wet, but will firm up as the cake cools on a rack. It is ready when it is *thoroughly* cooled. Cut into squares and serve right from the pan.

Stir-Crazy Chocolate-Cherry Cake

SERVES 12

Per serving: 155.8 Cal. / 1.26 g fat / 7% fat / 0.33 mg cholesterol

1¼ cups unbleached all-purpose flour
½ teaspoon baking soda
¾ cup plus 3 tablespoons sugar
⅓ cup cocoa
Pinch of salt
¼ plus ⅛ teaspoon almond extract
½ cup water
1 cup nonfat buttermilk
3 cups pitted and halved fresh sweet cherries, or 3 cups
  frozen unsweetened (unthawed) cherries
3 amaretti cookies, crumbled
½ teaspoon vanilla extract
Sprinkling of lemon juice

1. Preheat oven to 350° F.
2. Sift together the flour, baking soda, all but 1 tablespoon sugar, cocoa, and salt into a bowl. In a measuring cup, combine ¼ teaspoon almond extract, the water, and buttermilk. Pour the liquid mixture over the dry ingredients in the bowl. With a wooden spoon, stir the mixture together, using a gentle circular motion, until the dry ingredients are thoroughly incorporated into the liquid ones.
3. Pour and scrape the batter into a 13½-by-8½-inch ovenproof baking dish 2 inches deep. With a rubber spatula, evenly smooth the batter.
4. Combine the cherries, crumbled amaretti biscuits, remaining 1 tablespoon sugar, vanilla extract, remaining ⅛ teaspoon almond extract, and a sprinkling of lemon juice. Pour

and scatter this mixture in one even layer over the chocolate batter, leaving a ½-inch border all around.

5. Bake approximately 50 minutes. The edges of the cake will be set, and the surface, when pressed around the edges, will spring back. Cool on a rack. It is best when *thoroughly* cooled. Cut into squares and serve right from the pan.

Stir-Crazy Blueberry Cobbler

SERVES 8
MAKES A 10-INCH SQUARE COBBLER
Per serving: 189.3 Cal. / 0.23 g fat / 1% fat / 0.50 mg cholesterol

A stir-crazy batter *without* chocolate, spread in a square baking dish and topped with plenty of blueberries, makes a splendid cobbler.

BATTER
> *1⅓ cups plus 1 tablespoon unbleached all-purpose flour*
> *½ teaspoon baking soda*
> *½ cup sugar*
> *Pinch of salt*
> *1 teaspoon vanilla extract*
> *½ cup water*
> *1 cup nonfat buttermilk*

FRUIT MIX
> *5 cups fresh blueberries, or 5 cups unsweetened frozen (un-thawed) blueberries*
> *2 tablespoons sugar*
> *Pinch of salt*
> *Slivered zest of ½ orange*
> *Slivered zest of ½ lemon*

1. Preheat the oven to 350° F.
2. Sift together the flour, baking soda, sugar, and salt into a bowl. Combine the remaining batter ingredients in a measuring cup and pour the liquid over the flour. With a wooden spoon, gently stir the ingredients together, using a steady, circular motion. When the wet and dry ingredients are thoroughly amalgamated, pour and scrape the batter into a 10-inch square glass or ceramic baking dish. With a rubber spatula, evenly smooth the batter.
3. Combine the fruit mix ingredients and pour and scatter the mixture in an even layer over the top of the batter, leaving a ½-inch to 1-inch border.
4. Bake approximately 40 to 50 minutes. Cool on a rack.

I I I I VARIATIONS I I I I

Use 5 cups mixed raspberries, nectarines, and strawberries with 2 to 3 tablespoons sugar for the fruit mix.

Use 5 cups mixed raspberries, peaches, and cherries with 3 tablespoons sugar for the fruit mix.

Morning Coffee, Afternoon Tea

W ith morning coffee, afternoon tea, or at snack time, there is nothing like a mouthful of sweetness that packs a nutrient power punch along with its good taste.

Fruit-studded Spoonbread Muffins

MAKES 12 MUFFINS

Per muffin: 156.4 Cal. / 0.34 g fat / 2% fat / 0.33 mg cholesterol

This recipe (and the one that follows) is a cross between a muffin and spoonbread. The batter is made by cooking cornmeal in boiling water, stirring in a mixture of honey, buttermilk, and egg whites, and then folding in flour. The muffins are leavened by the baking soda and buttermilk. They are very tender and satisfying, like little fruit-studded puddings. They make a wonderful afterschool snack or breakfast.

> 1 cup finely diced dried peaches or apricots (use scissors)
> ¾ cup golden raisins
> 2 cups water
> 1 cup cornmeal
> 1 cup unbleached all-purpose flour
> 2 pinches of salt
> ½ teaspoon baking soda
> 3 egg whites
> 2 tablespoons mild honey
> 1 cup nonfat buttermilk

1. Simmer the dried fruit in 1 cup of the water until the water is almost gone. Cool.
2. Preheat the oven to 375° F.
3. Sift ½ cup cornmeal with the flour, the salt, and the soda. Set aside.
4. Beat the egg whites until foamy and stir in the honey and buttermilk. Set aside.
5. Bring the remaining cup of water to a boil in a nonstick saucepan. Pour the remaining ½ cup cornmeal into the water, whisking all the while. Switch to a wooden spoon and stir until the mixture is very smooth and clears the sides of the pan (this happens very quickly). Scrape the mixture into a large bowl.
6. Stir the fruit into the cooked cornmeal. Stir in the egg white–buttermilk mixture. Quickly fold in the sifted flour mixture. Do not overmix. Divide the batter among 12 foil muffin cups. Bake 25 to 35 minutes, until muffins are well risen, lightly browned, and feel firm but springy when lightly pressed. A cake tester will test clean. Cool on a rack.

Ginger-Pear Spoonbread Muffins

MAKES 12 MUFFINS
Per muffin: 123.8 Cal. / 0.13 g fat / 1% fat / 0.33 mg cholesterol

I've substituted farina cereal for the cornmeal in the previous recipe, and added some Indian spices. These muffins have a lovely, spicy fragrance.

1 cup finely diced dried pears (use scissors)
¾ cup golden raisins
2 cups water
4½ tablespoons quick farina cereal
1 cup unbleached all-purpose flour
1 teaspoon ground ginger
¼ teaspoon ground cinnamon
¼ teaspoon ground cardamom
2 pinches salt
½ teaspoon baking soda
3 egg whites
2 tablespoons mild honey
1 cup nonfat buttermilk

1. Preheat the oven to 375° F.
2. Simmer the dried fruit in 1 cup of the water until the water is almost gone. Cool.
3. Sift 1½ tablespoons of the farina cereal with the flour, spices, salt, and soda.
4. Beat the egg whites until foamy and stir in the honey and buttermilk.
5. Bring the remaining cup of water to a boil in a nonstick saucepan. Pour the remaining 3 tablespoons farina cereal into the water, whisking all the while. Simmer and stir until the mixture is smooth and thick. Scrape the mixture into a large bowl.

6. Stir the fruit into the cooked farina. Stir in the egg white–buttermilk mixture. Quickly and gently fold in the sifted flour mixture. Do not overmix. Divide the batter among 12 foil muffin cups. Bake 25 to 35 minutes, until muffins are well risen, browned, and feel firm yet springy when lightly pressed. A cake tester will test clean. Cool on a rack.

Citrus-scented Coffee Cake

SERVES 10 TO 12

MAKES ONE 12-INCH CAKE

Per serving ($^1/_{10}$): 166.0 Cal. / 0.41 g fat / 2% fat / 0.50 mg cholesterol
($^1/_{12}$): 138.3 Cal. / 0.34 g fat / 2% fat / 0.42 mg cholesterol

This coffee cake is made from a simple and very versatile soda bread dough. After trying this lemon version, try the soda bread variations that follow: a poppy seed loaf, or cranberry- or blueberry-studded bread.

3½ to 3¾ cups unbleached all-purpose flour
½ teaspoon ground cinnamon
⅛ teaspoon ground mace
1 teaspoon baking soda
Pinch of salt
Slivered zest of 1 orange
Slivered zest of 1 lemon
1¼ to 1½ cups nonfat buttermilk
2 tablespoons mild honey
1 teaspoon vanilla extract
½ teaspoon lemon extract
½ teaspoon orange extract

1.   Preheat oven to 400° F.

2.   Sift 3½ cups flour, the spices, soda, and salt into a big bowl.

3.   Make a well in the flour. Scatter the zests over the flour. Pour 1¼ cups buttermilk into the well, and drizzle the honey over the buttermilk. Dribble the extracts over the liquid. With a wooden spoon, gently stir the flour into the buttermilk. When the mixture forms large flakes, use your hands to work it very gently into a cohesive but very rough and shaggy mass. Don't overwork it. When it just begins to hold together into an untidy dough, it is ready. Add more buttermilk if the dough is too crumbly or more flour if too wet, but the dough should be a bit sticky.

4.   Lightly flour your hands and your work surface. Form the dough into a rough ball and flatten it. Roll it out into a circle (it doesn't have to be a perfect circle) that will fit into a 12-inch nonstick flan or quiche pan with a fluted rim. Lightly flour the top of the circle, and fold it into quarters. (Use a long flexible spatula to slip under the dough and fold it over.) Spray the pan lightly with nonstick vegetable spray. Center the dough in the pan and unfold. Build up the edges and press them against the edge of the pan to flute.

5.   Bake 20 to 25 minutes, until risen, lightly browned, and done. To test for doneness, carefully tip the coffee cake out of the pan and tap the bottom. It should sound hollow. Cool on a rack. (This cake is delicious either slightly warm or thoroughly cooled.) Serve topped with Honeyed Vanilla Cream (page 99) and cubed fresh fruit, berries, or a Fruit Compote (page 96).

Poppy Seed Loaf

S E R V E S 1 2

Per serving: 152.2 Cal. / 1.63 g fat / 10% fat / 0.42 mg cholesterol

3½ to 3¾ cups unbleached all-purpose flour
1 teaspoon baking soda
Pinch of salt
¼ cup poppy seeds
1¼ to 1½ cups nonfat buttermilk
2 tablespoons mild honey
1 teaspoon vanilla extract

1.   Preheat oven to 400° F.
2.   Sift 3½ cups flour, the soda, and salt into a big bowl.
Add the poppy seeds.
3.   Make a well in the flour. Pour 1¼ cups buttermilk into
the well, and drizzle the honey over the buttermilk. Dribble
the vanilla extract over the liquid. With a wooden spoon,
gently stir the flour into the buttermilk. When the mixture
forms large flakes, use your hands to work it very gently into
a cohesive but very rough and shaggy mass. Don't overwork
it. When it just begins to hold together into an untidy dough,
it is ready. Add more buttermilk if the dough is too crumbly
or more flour if too wet, but the dough should be a bit sticky.
4.   Pat and shape the dough into a loaf shape that will fit
into an 8-by-5-by-3-inch (6½-cup) nonstick or ceramic loaf
pan. Spray the pan lightly with nonstick vegetable spray. Put
the dough into the pan.
5.   Bake 30 to 35 minutes, until risen and well browned.
When the loaf is done, it will sound hollow if you tip it out
and thump your knuckle on the bottom.

Cranberry-Nut Bread

SERVES 12
Per serving: 179.2 Cal. / 2.67 g fat / 13% fat / 0.42 mg cholesterol

3½ to 3¾ cups unbleached all-purpose flour
1 teaspoon baking soda
Pinch of salt
*2 cups cranberries (frozen cranberries work fine; do not
    thaw them)*
2 tablespoons orange marmalade
2 ounces pine nuts
1¼ to 1½ cups nonfat buttermilk
2 tablespoons mild honey
1 teaspoon vanilla extract

1.   Preheat oven to 350° F.
2.   Sift 3½ cups flour, the soda, and salt into a big bowl.
3.   Toss the cranberries with the marmalade, then toss them
into the flour. Sprinkle on the pine nuts.
4.   Make a well in the flour. Pour 1¼ cups buttermilk into
the well, and drizzle the honey over the buttermilk. Dribble
the vanilla extract over the liquid. With a wooden spoon,
gently stir the flour into the buttermilk. When the mixture
forms large flakes, use your hands to work it very gently into
a cohesive but very rough, shaggy mass. Don't overwork it.
Add more buttermilk if the dough is too crumbly or more
flour if too wet, but the dough should be a bit sticky. When
the dough comes together in a mass, knead it very slightly
3 or 4 turns right in the bowl. Line a baking sheet with baking
parchment.
5.   Form the dough into a plump round and center it on the
sheet. If it is hard to handle because it is too sticky, dust it

and your hands with a bit of flour. Cut a cross on the top of the loaf.

6.   Bake 50 to 60 minutes, until done. A cake tester will test clean, and the loaf will sound hollow if you tip it out and thump the bottom with your knuckle. Cool on a rack.

Mincemeat Coffee Cake

SERVES 8 TO 10
MAKES ONE 10½-INCH SQUARE CAKE
Per serving (⅛): 354.1 Cal. / 0.24 g ft / 1% fat / 0.50 mg cholesterol
(¹/₁₀): 283.3 Cal. / 0.20 g fat / 1% fat / 0.40 mg cholesterol

Here is a coffee cake that is a powerpack of nutrients and fiber. And, of course, very good to eat.

MINCEMEAT
  MAKES 2½ CUPS
  ¼ cup golden raisins
  4 cups mixed dried fruit (dried apricots, apples, figs, prunes, pears), diced
  1 cup orange juice
  1 cup apple juice
  1 tablespoon superfine sugar
  ¼ teaspoon lemon extract
  ½ cinnamon stick
  Grated zest of ½ lemon
  Grated zest of ½ orange

1.   Combine the raisins, diced fruit, orange juice, and apple juice in a 10½-inch square glass or ceramic baking dish. Allow to soak for 1 hour.

Tea time (*clockwise from top*): Chocolate Chewies, Chocolate Meringues, Thumbprint Cookies, Fruit-Studded Spoonbread Muffins, Stir-Crazy Banana Fudge Cake with Honeyed Vanilla Cream, and Plum-Peach Compote

Chocoholics unite (*clockwise from lower left*): Chocolate-Almond Pie, Chocolate Roulade filled with Orange-Ricotta, Milk Chocolate Ice Cream, Chocolate Sorbet, and Chocolate Pudding

The soup is *supposed* to be cold! Peach–Raspberry Soup with
Peach Sorbet (*bottom*), Cold Blueberry Soup with Blueberry
Sorbet (*left*), and Hot and Cold Pineapple (*right*)

Morning coffee (*clockwise from upper right*): Blueberry Compote, Peach Charlotte, Blueberry Batter Pudding, Peach Batter Pudding, Cherry Batter Pudding, and Bagels with quark

Life's little aggravations are soothed by frequent doses
of cheesecake (*from right to left*): Amaretti Cheese Pie
and Pineapple Cheese Pie

For an afternoon tea-time treat in the garden, spread
your biscuits or scones with Fruit Compote
and Honeyed Vanilla Cream

Winter comfort (*clockwise from bottom left*): Apple–Raisin
Flan, Winter Pudding, and Fruit Soufflé

Delights of summer (*clockwise from lower left*): No-Sugar, No-Cook Summer Pudding, Cherries in strawberry coulis, Strawberry Frozen Yogurt, and strawberry-flavored *coeur à la crème* with strawberry coulis

You may have your cake and stay slim too! Angel Cake
and Black and White Angel Cake

Irresistible sweets *(clockwise from bottom)*: Citrus-Scented Coffee Cake topped with Fruit Compote, Orange-Lychee Bread Pudding, Rum-Raisin Cheese Pie with Blueberry Compote, and Honeyed Vanilla Cream

Can she bake a cherry pie? Of course, she can! (*right to left*):
Cherry-Peach Flan and Pear-Raspberry Flan

Be a soda jerk in your spare time (*clockwise from upper left*):
Chocolate Milkshake, Vanilla Milkshake, mango rickey with
Peach Sorbet, raspberry rickey with Melon Sorbet, hot fudge
sundae made with Vanilla Ice Cream and Hot Chocolate Sauce,
and a Banana Split.

2. Preheat the oven to 350° F.

3. At the end of the hour, stir in the sugar, lemon extract, cinnamon stick, lemon zest, and orange zest. Cover the dish and bake for 1 hour. Refrigerate until needed (it keeps for weeks).

COFFEE CAKE BATTER

1½ cups unbleached all-purpose flour
½ teaspoon baking soda
½ cup sugar
Pinch of salt
1 teaspoon vanilla extract
Grated zest of ½ orange
Grated zest of ½ lemon
½ teaspoon cinnamon
½ cup water
1 cup nonfat buttermilk

1. Preheat oven to 350° F.

2. Sift the flour, baking soda, sugar, and salt into a bowl. Combine the remaining batter ingredients in a 2-cup measuring cup. Pour mixture over the flour. With a wooden spoon, gently stir the ingredients together, using a steady, circular motion. When the dry and wet ingredients are thoroughly amalgamated, pour and scrape the batter into a 10½-inch square ceramic or glass baking dish. With a rubber spatula, evenly smooth the batter in the dish.

3. Scatter the Mincemeat in an even layer over the top of the batter, leaving a ½-inch border.

4. Bake 30 to 40 minutes, until the bordering dough is golden and firm. If the fruit starts to brown before the cake is done, cover it loosely with parchment paper. Cool in the pan on a rack.

Blueberry Bread

SERVES 12

Per serving: 159.8 Cal. / 0.33 g fat / 2% fat / 0.42 mg cholesterol

3½ to 3¾ cups unbleached all-purpose flour
1 teaspoon baking soda
Pinch of salt
2 cups blueberries (frozen blueberries work fine; do not
* thaw them)*
2 tablespoons lemon marmalade
1¼ to 1½ cups nonfat buttermilk
2 tablespoons mild honey
1 teaspoon vanilla extract

1. Preheat oven to 350° F.
2. Sift 3½ cups flour, the soda, and salt into a big bowl.
3. Toss the blueberries with the marmalade, then toss them
into the flour.
4. Make a well in the flour. Pour 1¼ cups buttermilk into
the well, and drizzle the honey over the buttermilk. Dribble
the vanilla extract over the liquid. With a wooden spoon,
gently stir the flour into the buttermilk. When the mixture
forms large flakes, use your hands to work it very gently into
a cohesive but very rough shaggy mass. Don't overwork it.
Add more buttermilk if the dough is too crumbly or more
flour if too wet, but the dough should be a bit sticky. When
the dough comes together in a mass, knead it very lightly 3
or 4 turns right in the bowl. Line a baking sheet with baking
parchment.
5. Form the dough into a plump round and center it on the
sheet. If it is hard to handle because it is too sticky, dust it
and your hands with a bit of flour. Cut a cross on the top of
the loaf.

6. Bake 50 to 60 minutes, until done. A cake tester will test clean, and if you thump the bottom with your knuckle, it will sound hollow. Cool on a rack.

Fig Bread

S E R V E S   1 2

Per serving: 271.1 Cal. / 0.84 g fat / 3% fat / 0.19 mg cholesterol

Serve this citrus- and vanilla-scented fig-filled bread in wedges for breakfast, snack time, tea, picnics, or as a special treat in packed lunches. If the figs are left whole, the cross section of plump fig slices in each wedge looks very dramatic. Chopped, the figs make a more compact filling. Both are delicious.

> *¼ ounce yeast cake, or 1½ teaspoons active dry yeast*
> *1¾ cups warm water (100° F to 115° F)*
> *1 tablespoon mild honey*
> *1 cup instant potato flakes*
> *3 tablespoons nonfat dry milk*
> *Approximately 3 cups unbleached all-purpose flour*
> *Slivered zest of 1 orange*
> *Slivered zest of 1 lemon*
> *Pinch of salt*
> *1 teaspoon vanilla extract*
> *1 batch Glazed Figs (recipe follows), stems removed*

1. Combine the yeast with ½ cup warm water and the honey in a 2-cup measuring cup. Stir with a fork or tiny whisk to dissolve the yeast.
2. Combine the potato flakes, dry milk, 3 cups flour, zests,

salt, and vanilla in the container of the food processor. Stir the remaining water into the yeast mixture. Turn on the processor and pour the yeast mixture gradually through the feed tube. Stop to scrape the mixture down. Process until the mixture forms a dough. Remove to a floured board, and knead, adding flour as necessary, until the mixture forms a smooth, not too sticky dough. It is kneaded sufficiently when a finger indentation springs back. Form the dough into a ball, lightly dust the dough with flour, and put it into a bowl, loosely covered with plastic wrap. Leave it to rise in a warm place until doubled in bulk, approximately 1½ hours.

3. Punch the dough down and knead it a few times on a lightly floured surface to expel the gas. If it is very sticky, knead in a bit of flour, but avoid adding too much, or the dough will be heavy. Cut the dough into 2 equal pieces, form each piece into a smooth ball, and let rest while you preheat the oven to 400° F.

4. On a lightly floured surface, roll 1 ball of dough into a circle approximately 10 inches in diameter. Put the dough on a nonstick baking sheet that has been lightly dusted with flour or cornmeal. Spread the figs and all their juices over the dough, leaving a 1- to 2-inch border all around. Roll out the second piece of dough so that it is a little bigger than the first circle. Drape it over the fig-filled base and tuck the edges under all around. Pinch closed.

5. Bake 20 to 35 minutes. For the last 10 minutes or so of baking, turn the loaf upside down, so that it browns evenly. It is done when it is golden and a knuckle thump on the bottom produces a hollow sound. Cool on a rack.

Glazed Figs

MAKES 2½ CUPS

Per ½ cup: 253.6 Cal. / 1.07 g fat / 4% fat / 0 mg cholesterol

Dried figs, simmered in vermouth that has been spiked with orange liqueur, citrus juice and zests, and flavored with cinnamon and vanilla, are delicious on their own or as a filling in Fig Bread. The glazed figs will keep in the refrigerator, well covered, for weeks.

> 1 pound ready-to-eat (presoaked) dried figs
> 1 cup sweet vermouth
> 1 tablespoon orange liqueur (Grand Marnier or Cointreau)
> Juice and slivered zest of ½ orange
> Slivered zest of ½ lemon
> 1 cinnamon stick
> 1 vanilla bean
> ½ cup water

1. Combine all ingredients in a nonreactive saucepan.
2. Simmer briskly, stirring occasionally, until the liquid has reduced to a thick syrupy glaze and the figs are plumply tender.

Bagels

MAKES 16 TO 18

Per bagel (¹⁄₁₆): 156.3 Cal. / 0.41 g fat / 2% fat / 0 mg cholesterol
(¹⁄₁₈): 139.0 Cal. / 0.37 g fat / 2% fat / 0 mg cholesterol

A bagel is a dense, round roll with a hole in the middle. A split bagel (see box) spread with quark or smoothed-out nonfat cottage cheese, a Fruit Compote (page 96), or Honeyed Vanilla or Almond Cream (pages 99, 101) will light up your morning. If you live in a bagel-free zone, it's nice to know that you can easily make your own, and then freeze what you don't use in a day. A frozen bagel, wrapped in foil and placed in a 400° F oven, takes 15 to 20 minutes to thaw. It emerges piping hot and tastes freshly baked.

Two ¼-ounce packages active dry yeast
2 cups warm water (100° to 115° F)
3 tablespoons kosher salt, plus additional for sprinkling
5½ to 6 cups bread flour
¼ cup sugar
2 egg whites
1 tablespoon water
Poppy seeds
Sesame seeds

1. Combine the yeast and warm water in a large bowl. Stir with a fork or a small whisk. Add 1 tablespoon salt.
2. Stir in 5 cups of flour, 1 cup at a time. Use a whisk until the mixture becomes stiff, then switch to a wooden spoon.
3. Use a handful of the remaining flour to flour your work surface. Turn the dough out and knead rhythmically and vigorously, adding more flour as you knead, until the dough is smooth, springy, nonsticky, and elastic. This dough should be quite stiff. It is kneaded sufficently when you can poke it with your finger and the indentation springs back. Total kneading time will be 10 to 15 minutes.
4. Cover the dough with a cloth and let it rest while you wash, dry, and lightly flour the bowl. Knead the dough a few more turns, then form it into a ball and place in the bowl. Dust the top lightly with flour. Cover the bowl and put it in a warm, draft-free place until it doubles in bulk (about 1 hour). It has risen sufficiently when you can poke a finger in the dough and the hole remains after about 5 minutes. (Poke

very gently or the dough will collapse.)

5.   When the dough is doubled, flour your fist and punch the dough down. Knead a few times, then allow to rest for a few minutes. Divide the dough into 16 to 18 equal pieces. As you work with one piece, keep the remainder covered with a kitchen towel. Spread another towel out on a clean work surface.

6.   Roll each piece of dough between your hands to form a smooth ball. Flatten slightly and use your thumb to form a hole in the center about 1 inch in diameter. Place finished circles on the towel-covered surface.

7.   Cover bagels lightly with plastic wrap and let rise for 10 to 30 minutes, until puffy but not quite doubled. In the meantime, preheat the oven to 450° F. In a large soup pot combine 5 quarts water, the sugar, and the remaining 2 tablespoons salt. Bring to a boil. Cut parchment paper to fit one large or two small baking sheets. Place the paper on sheets and lightly coat with nonstick vegetable spray.

8.   Adjust the water bath to remain at a gentle boil. Four or five at a time, drop the bagels into the water. Cook for 3 minutes, turn with tongs, and cook for 2 to 3 minutes on the second side. Remove with a skimmer or slotted spoon and place briefly back on the towel to drain. Place on the baking sheet.

9.   Beat the egg whites with 1 tablespoon water. Brush the top of each bagel with this mixture, and sprinkle with kosher salt, poppy seeds, or sesame seeds, if desired.

10.   Bake in the preheated oven for 20 to 30 minutes, until golden brown and crusty. Remove from the baking sheets. (You may have to peel off the paper.) Let cool on racks. These freeze beautifully. As soon as they have cooled, seal in plastic bags and freeze. To reheat, place frozen bagels, wrapped in foil, on a baking sheet. Bake in a 350° F oven for 15 minutes.

NOTE: The boiled, *unbaked* bagels may be frozen at the end of Step 8. Let them cool, wrap them well, and freeze until needed. At serving time, place the frozen bagels on a parchment-covered baking sheet that has been lightly sprayed with a nonstick vegetable spray. Bake in a 400° F oven 40 to 45 minutes, until brown, crusty, and done. If you know you're going to freeze bagels don't bake them first. Unbaked bagels that have been frozen and then baked are even better and crustier than baked bagels that have been frozen and reheated.

FIRST, SPLIT YOUR BAGEL

Never use a knife to split a bagel. Proper bagel behavior demands a fork. With the tines of a fork, perforate the bagel all around its outer perimeter. Then, separate the bagel into halves along the dotted line. When bagels are halved in this manner, the texture of the inner surface of each bagel half will be rough and absolutely delicious, whether spread with smoothed-out cottage cheese or quark, one of the honeyed creams, or fruit compote.

Prune Butter

MAKES APPROXIMATELY 2 ¼ CUPS
Per tbsp.: 12.8 Cal. / 0.23 g fat / 16% fat / .89 mg cholesterol

Prune butter contains no butter, but it spreads like butter, and will do wonderful things to your breakfast toast.

One 9-ounce package ready-to-eat (presoaked) prunes, diced
8 ounces low-fat ricotta cheese
¼ teaspoon vanilla extract
Juice of ¼ lemon
⅛ teaspoon ground mace
⅛ teaspoon ground cinnamon
⅛ teaspoon ground allspice

Put all the ingredients into the bowl of a food processor and blend until smooth. Taste and blend in a bit more seasoning if you feel it needs it. Store in the refrigerator until needed.

Fig Butter   ☐

MAKES APPROXIMATELY 2 ¼ CUPS
Per tbsp.: 22.5 Cal. / 0.28 g fat / 11% fat / .78 mg cholesterol

Use fig butter to fill a Roulade (page 54) and you have a low-fat and very sophisticated version of the childhood classic, the fig newton.

One 9-ounce package ready-to-eat (presoaked) figs,
*   stems removed*
1 cup low-fat ricotta cheese
¼ teaspoon vanilla extract
Sprinkling of granulated sugar substitute, to taste
Few drops of fresh lemon juice

1.   Dice the figs. Put them into the container of a food processor with the ricotta and vanilla. Blend until almost smooth.

‖‖

2. Add the granulated sugar substitute to taste (if any is needed at all) and a few drops of fresh lemon juice. Process until perfectly smooth. Taste and adjust flavorings, then process once more to blend. Store in the refrigerator until needed.

Fruit Compotes

EACH RECIPE MAKES 3 TO 3 ¾ CUPS OF COMPOTE

Fresh fruit compotes make great spreads for toast and bagels. They're easy to make: The basic recipe can be adapted to any seasonal fruit that takes your fancy. The amount of sugar needed depends on the sweetness or tartness of the particular batch of fruit. You can always use a moderate amount of sugar, and then adjust the sweetness with low-Calorie sweetener after the compote has cooled.

CHERRY
Per tbsp.: 16.88 Cal. / 0.29 g fat / 16% fat / 0 mg cholesterol

5 cups stemmed, pitted, halved sweet cherries (stem and pit over a cup so that you catch all the juices)
2 tablespoons superfine sugar
Pinch of salt
1 tablespoon cornstarch
2 tablespoons fresh orange juice
Slivered zest of ½ small lemon
Slivered zest of ½ small orange
½ teaspoon vanilla extract

Combine all ingredients in a nonreactive saucepan. Cook slowly on top of the stove until thick and juicy. The fruit should be tender, but retain its shape. Cool.

PEACH
Per tbsp.: 10.58 Cal. / 0 g fat / 0% fat / 0 mg cholesterol

> *5 cups pitted, chunked, unpeeled peaches (cut into chunks*
> *over a cup so that you catch all the juices)*
> *2 tablespoons superfine sugar*
> *Pinch of salt*
> *1 tablespoon cornstarch*
> *2 tablespoons fresh orange juice*
> *Slivered zest of ½ small lemon*
> *Slivered zest of ½ small orange*
> *½ teaspoon vanilla extract*

Combine all ingredients in a nonreactive saucepan. Cook slowly on top of the stove until thick and juicy. The fruit should be tender, but retain its shape. Cool.

PLUM-PEACH
Per tbsp.: 13.72 Cal. / 0 g fat / 0% fat / 0 mg cholesterol

> *5 cups pitted, chunked, unpeeled plums (about 1 pound*
> *12 ounces)*
> *2½ cups pitted, chunked, unpeeled peaches (pit and chunk*
> *the fruits over a bowl so that you catch their juices)*
> *1 tablespoon cornstarch*
> *Pinch of salt*
> *4 to 5 tablespoons light brown sugar*
> *Slivered zest of ½ lemon*
> *Slivered zest of ½ orange*
> *1 teaspoon vanilla extract*
> *3 tablespoons fresh orange juice*

Combine all ingredients in a nonreactive saucepan. Cook slowly on top of the stove until thick and juicy. The fruit should be tender, but retain its shape. Cool.

||||||||||||||||||||||||||||||||||||||||||||||||||||||||||||||||||||||||||

APRICOT-PEACH
Per tbsp.: 11.03 Cal. / 0 g fat / 0% fat / 0 mg cholesterol

3¾ cups apricots, unpeeled, pitted, and quartered
1¼ cups peaches, unpeeled, pitted, and quartered (pit and
chunk the fruits over a cup so that you catch their juices)
1 tablespoon cornstarch
Pinch of salt
3 to 5 tablespoons light brown sugar
Slivered zest of ½ orange
Slivered zest of ½ lemon
1 teaspoon vanilla extract
1 tablespoon Amaretto di Sarrono

Combine all ingredients in a nonreactive saucepan. Cook slowly on top of the stove until thick and juicy. The fruit should be tender, but retain its shape. Cool.

BLUEBERRY
Per tbsp.: 11.89 Cal. / 0 g fat / 0% fat / 0 mg cholesterol

3¾ cups blueberries, rinsed and dried
3 to 4 tablespoons superfine sugar
Pinch of salt
1 tablespoon cornstarch
½ tablespoon lemon juice
Pinch of ground cinnamon
Pinch of freshly grated nutmeg

Combine all ingredients in a nonreactive saucepan. Cook slowly on top of the stove until thick and juicy. The fruit should be tender, but retain its shape. Cool.

Honeyed Vanilla Cream ◔

MAKES 2 ¼ CUPS

Per tbsp.: 13.1 Cal. / 0 g fat / 0% fat / 0.04 mg cholesterol

Honey and the pulp of vanilla bean give fragrant character to smoothed-out cottage cheese. Use dollops of the aromatic cream on toast or bagels, fruit and berries, or on slices of Angel Cake (pages 65–69) or Stir-Crazy Cake (pages 70–76).

> *1 pound 2 ounces nonfat* fromage blanc, *quark, or*
>   *cottage cheese*
> *1 tablespoon nonfat dry milk (if you are using*
>   *cottage cheese)*
> *1 vanilla bean*
> *2 tablespoons mild honey*

1. If you are using cottage cheese, put it with the dry milk in the food processor or blender. With a small, sharp knife, split the vanilla bean lengthwise. With the tip of the knife, scrape out the soft aromatic inside pulp of both halves into the cottage cheese. (Save the scraped pod to store in a jar of granulated sugar substitute or a canister of sugar. It will impart its fragrance to the sweetener.)

2. Add the honey to the cottage cheese. Process until well blended. Store in the refrigerator.

3. If you are using *fromage blanc* or quark, stir the vanilla pulp and honey in with a small whisk.

♡ Use granulated sugar substitute instead of honey.

A GIFT FROM THE BEES

We all know that honey is produced by bees, but how exactly is it made? A bee collects nectar from flowers and transports it—in the bee's honey sac—to the hive. As the bee rushes from flower to hive, its digestive fluids begin to break down the nectar's sugars. At the hive, the bee regurgitates the nectar into the mouths of young bees. The young bees breathe on the nectar to concentrate it; at the same time their secretions cause further changes in its chemical structure. Finally, the nectar is stored in special cells of the hive, where it concentrates even further, and becomes thick, sweet honey. There are as many varieties as there are kinds of flower nectars for bees to feast upon. Wild thyme honey, orange blossom, sage, rosemary, apple blossom—the names themselves are intoxicating.

Honeyed Almond Cream ⏲

MAKES 2 ¼ CUPS
Per tbsp.: 13.51 Cal. / 0 g fat / 0% fat / 0.04 mg cholesterol

*1 pound 2 ounces nonfat fromage blanc, quark, or
  cottage cheese*
1 teaspoon vanilla extract
½ teaspoon almond extract
*1 tablespoon nonfat dry milk (if you are using
  cottage cheese)*
2 tablespoons mild honey

If you are using cottage cheese, combine all the ingredients in a food processor or blender. Process until thoroughly blended. If you are using quark or *fromage blanc,* stir the extracts and the honey in with a small whisk. Store in the refrigerator.

Thumbprint Cookies

MAKES 20 COOKIES
Per cookie: 23.8 Cal. / 0 g fat / 0% fat / 0 mg cholesterol

An American food writer living and working in England traverses a minefield of possible confusions every working moment. What an English person calls a scone, an American calls a biscuit. Well, the English have their biscuits too, but in America they're called cookies. So the recipe that follows is for crunchy little thumbprint cookies, but the English call them thumbprint *biscuits*. You can eat them plain, or pipe or spoon into the thumbprint depressions one of the Slim Cuisine creams or butters—Chestnut-Chocolate Cream (page 170), Honeyed Vanilla Cream (page 99), Fig Butter (page 95), or Chocolate "Butter" (page 163). Eat these biscuits or cookies with tea or coffee along with your biscuits or scones. Whichever way you refer to these delightful little cream-filled morsels, you are sure to enjoy them.

> *½ cup plus 1 tablespoon amaretti cookies, crushed*
> *½ cup plus 1½ tablespoons Grape-Nuts, crushed*
> *2 egg whites*

1. Preheat oven to 350° F.
2. Combine all the ingredients thoroughly in a bowl. Choose a nonstick baking sheet and line it with baking parchment. Roll 1-teaspoon measures of the mixture into balls. Flatten each ball onto the nonstick baking sheet. Using your thumb, make a depression with a raised edge in each cookie. Bake 18 to 20 minutes (depending on the humidity), until dry and crisp. Cool on a rack.

▌▌▌▌ VARIATION ▌▌▌▌

Chocolate Chewies
MAKES 24 COOKIES
Per cookie: 19.27 Cal. / 0.02 g fat / 1% fat / 0 mg cholesterol
Add a little cocoa powder, forget the thumbprint, and you have chewy little chocolate cookies.

> *¾ cup crushed amaretti cookies (approximately 12)*
> *⅓ cup plus 1 tablespoon Grape-Nuts, crushed*
> *2 egg whites, lightly beaten*
> *2 teaspoons cocoa powder, sifted*

1. Preheat the oven to 350° F. Line a baking sheet with parchment paper.
2. Combine the crushed amaretti cookies and the cereal with the lightly beaten egg whites.
3. Add the cocoa and mix. Drop the mixture onto the baking sheet in 1-teaspoon dollops.
4. Bake approximately 18 to 20 minutes, until dry. Remove from the tray and cool on a rack.

Meringue Cookies

MAKES 100 COOKIES
Per cookie: 5.98 Cal. / 0 g fat / 0% fat / 0 mg cholesterol

If you bake these on a humid or rainy day, they will never quite dry out—there will be that slight sticky-gooeyness in the center. Of course, many people prefer them that way.

> 3 egg whites, at room temperature
> Pinch of cream of tartar
> Pinch of salt
> ¾ cup sugar
> 1 teaspoon vanilla extract

1. Preheat oven to 225° F.
2. In an electric mixer, beat egg whites with cream of tartar and salt until foamy. Increase mixer speed. Beat, adding sugar 1 to 2 tablespoons at a time, until meringue is shiny and stiff and firm peaks hold. Fold in vanilla.
3. Line two baking sheets with parchment paper. Drop batter on sheets by the half-teaspoon, 1 inch apart. Bake for 1½ hours.

4.   Turn the oven off. Leave cookies in the oven for at least 3 hours. (They may stay in overnight.) Do not open the door until the time is up. Store in an airtight container.

Chocolate Meringue Cookies with Wheaty Bits

M A K E S   6 0   C O O K I E S
Per cookie: 12.33 Cal. / 0.05 g fat / 3% fat / 0 mg cholesterol

> *3 egg whites, at room temperature*
> *Pinch of cream of tartar*
> *Pinch of salt*
> *¾ cup sugar*
> *1 teaspoon vanilla extract*
> *¼ cup cocoa powder, sifted*
> *1¼ cups unsweetened puffed wheat*

1.   Preheat oven to 250° F.
2.   In an electric mixer, beat egg whites with cream of tartar and salt until foamy. Increase mixer speed. Beat, adding sugar 1 to 2 tablespoons at a time, until whites are shiny and stiff and hold firm peaks. Fold in the vanilla, cocoa, and unsweetened puffed wheat.
3.   Line two baking sheets with baking parchment. Drop batter on sheets by the teaspoon, 1 inch apart. Bake for 1½ hours.
4.   Turn the oven off. Leave cookies in the oven for at *least* 3 hours. (Overnight is better.) Do not open the door until the time is up.

COLD COMFORT

I SCREAM, YOU SCREAM,
WE ALL SCREAM FOR ICE CREAM

Ice cream is often considered a treat for children only, but historically speaking, nothing is further from the truth. Ice cream came to Europe in the thirteenth century, when Marco Polo came home from the Chinese court bearing a recipe for water ices. The Italian aristocracy loved the icy confection, but it wasn't until the fourteenth century that someone thought to add milk and eggs to the basic recipe. In 1533 the youth who was to become France's King Henry II married the young Italian Catherine de Médicis. Catherine brought a culinary dowry to France that included sweetbreads, veal, artichoke hearts—and ice cream. For each day of the wedding celebration, the chefs prepared a new flavor. French royalty reveled in the ice cream, but it didn't reach the plain folk until 1660, when a Sicilian named Francesco Procopio opened the Café Procope in Paris.

By the eighteenth century ice cream reached England, and soon after, America. George Washington purchased two ice cream pots: pewter vessels in which the ingredients were combined, beaten by hand, and agitated in a surrounding bath of ice and salt, until the proper creamy, frozen consistency was achieved. But it took a woman to really get things going. In 1846, an American named Nancy Johnson invented the hand-cranked ice cream freezer. In 1851 in Baltimore, the first commercial ice cream business was established; in 1874 in Philadelphia, the ice cream soda was born; and in 1904, at the St. Louis World's Fair, a quick thinking Syrian-American waffle vendor invented the ice cream cone. Ice cream, which had begun as ultrasophisticated gastronomic exotica in the royal courts of Europe, now belonged to everyone, especially to the children.

HOMEMADE ICE CREAM

You can buy expensive and elegant machines that contain their own freezing units. Pour in your ice cream mix, push the button, and in about half an hour your ice cream is ready. There are also elegant machines available that are not expensive at all. They do not contain their own freezing unit, but are designed to go directly into your home freezer. Pour in the ice cream mix and you can have homemade ice cream in half an hour. With your own machine, you can have ice cream whenever you like, as often as you like, and you can control exactly what goes into it. If you have no machine, but you have a freezer, you can still make a very decent homemade ice cream by the still-freeze method (instructions follow).

Commercial ice creams contain plenty of sugar and much too much fat for a prudent health-conscious (or fat-prone) person to eat. My ice creams are made with skim milk. (Technically they are not ice "creams." They contain no cream or whole milk.) The addition of nonfat dry milk to the skim milk adds an amazing richness to the ice cream. They have a pure, vivid creaminess that will delight you. They are at their creamiest right after they are made, or stored in the freezer for an hour or so. If they stay frozen overnight, they turn fairly hard. In that case, leave them on the counter for 15 minutes or so before scooping.

THE STILL-FREEZE METHOD

To prepare ice creams without a machine, pour the ice cream mixture into a metal bowl and place the bowl in the coldest part of the freezer. Put a metal whisk or the detachable beaters from an electric mixer into the freezer as well. Pull out the bowl and whisk or beaters every 2 hours or so, and thoroughly whisk or beat the partially frozen mixture to break up the ice crystals. By the time you've done this three times, the ice cream should be ready. Store, covered, in the freezer. Ice cream prepared by this method will be somewhat less creamy than the machine method—more of an ice *milk* than an ice *cream*—but still very good considering the zero fat content.

Vanilla Ice Cream

MAKES 3 CUPS
Per ½ cup: 105.0 Cal. / 0 g fat / 0% fat / 2.08 mg cholesterol

Today's quality vanilla ice creams are marred by their too-high butterfat content, which destroys the purity of taste and leaves a cloying, underlying fattiness on the palate. Inexpensive vanilla ice creams are ruined by synthetic vanilla flavoring (very harsh and unpleasant) and the stabilizers and fillers used in the product (read the labels next time you pass the supermarket freezer case). My vanilla ice cream is a return to innocence: virtually no butterfat, no stabilizers, pure vanilla.

> *2 cups skim milk*
> *6 to 8 tablespoons nonfat dry milk*
> *½ cup sugar*
> *1 teaspoon vanilla extract, or the scrapings from 1 vanilla*
>   *bean (page 8)*

1. Combine all ingredients and mix until the sugar is dissolved.
2. Pour into the canister of an ice cream machine and proceed according to the manufacturer's directions, or use the still-freeze method (page 109).

Milk Chocolate Ice Cream

MAKES APPROXIMATELY 3 CUPS
Per ½ cup: 129.3 Cal. / 0.60 g fat / 4% fat / 2.33 mg cholesterol

I have to admit it: I love vanilla ice cream, but I hear that chocolate calling to me.

> *½ cup nonfat dry milk*
> *½ cup sugar*
> *⅓ cup cocoa powder*
> *2 cups skim milk*
> *1 teaspoon vanilla extract*

1. Sift the dry milk, sugar, and cocoa into the skim milk. Whisk lightly, then pour into the blender jar and blend well.

2. Pour into a heavy-bottomed saucepan. Heat gently, stirring, until just beginning to bubble around the edges. Simmer gently, stirring for a minute or two. Stir in the vanilla. Pour the mixture into a bowl and cool.

3. Freeze in an ice cream maker according to the manufacturer's instructions, or use the still-freeze method (page 109).

Deep Dark Chocolate Ice Cream

MAKES 3 CUPS

Per ½ cup: 149.6 Cal. / 2.32 g fat / 14% fat / 6.37 mg cholesterol

Chocoholics, take note: This is a deep, meaningful chocolate experience. It will strike you speechless. To call it *intensely chocolatey* does not begin to describe its impact.

> *1 cup low-fat ricotta cheese*
> *1 cup skim milk*
> *1 recipe Hot Buttermilk Fudge Sauce, cooled (page 170)*

1. Combine the ricotta and milk in the food processor and process until perfectly smooth. Process in the Hot Buttermilk Fudge Sauce.

2. Freeze in an ice cream maker according to the manufacturer's instructions, or use the still-freeze method (page 109).

Coffee Ice Cream ❈

MAKES 3 CUPS

Per ½ cup: 95.78 Cal. / 0 g fat / 0% fat / 1.67 mg cholesterol

Use best quality filter or espresso coffee only. If you are anticaffeine, use filter water-process decaffeinated coffee. Try serving a coffee cup sundae: a pool of Hot Chocolate Sauce (page 121), a couple of scoops of coffee ice cream, and a sprinkled topping of mixed crunchy toasted wheat cereal and crumbled amaretti cookies. Serve in your prettiest coffee cups.

> 1 cup strong coffee
> 1 cup skim milk
> ½ cup nonfat dry milk
> ½ cup sugar
> ½ teaspoon vanilla extract

1. Combine all ingredients and mix until the sugar is dissolved.
2. Pour into the canister of an ice cream machine and proceed according to the manufacturer's directions, or use the still-freeze method (page 109).

Amaretti Ice Cream ❈

MAKES 2½ CUPS

Per ½ cup: 74.9 Cal. / 0.03 g fat / 0% fat / 2.80 mg cholesterol

Crunchy amaretti cookies crumbled into basic vanilla make a delicious almond-haunted ice cream. Like all Slim Cuisine ice creams, the texture is very creamy but without the slightest bit of cloying fattiness.

> 2 cups skim milk
> ½ cup nonfat dry milk
> 1 tablespoon sugar
> ¼ teaspoon almond extract
> 1 teaspoon vanilla extract
> 4 amaretti cookies, crushed

1.   Combine the first five ingredients and half the crushed amaretti crumbs, and mix until the sugar is dissolved.
2.   Pour into the canister of an ice cream machine and proceed according to the manufacturer's directions, or use the still-freeze method (page 109).
3.   Sprinkle in half the remaining amaretti cookie crumbs just before the ice cream is ready, and fold the rest of the cookie crumbs into the ice cream at the end.

Grape-Nuts Ice Cream

MAKES APPROXIMATELY 3 CUPS
Per ½ cup: 103.4 Cal. / 0.02 g fat / 0% fat / 2.33 mg cholesterol

Here, the toasted wheat and barley cereal contributes a most pleasing gentle crunchiness to brown sugar–and–cinnamon-flavored ice cream.

> 2 cups skim milk
> ½ cup nonfat dry milk
> ⅓ cup sugar
> 1 teaspoon vanilla extract
> 2 tablespoons Grape-Nuts
> 1 teaspoon ground cinnamon
> ½ tablespoon light brown sugar

1. Combine all ingredients and mix until the sugar is dissolved.
2. Pour into the canister of an ice cream machine and proceed according to the manufacturer's directions, or use the still-freeze method (page 109).

IIII VARIATION IIII

Mincemeat Ice Cream: When the ice cream is almost done, add 2 to 3 tablespoons of Mincemeat (page 86).

Banana Ice Cream

MAKES 6 CUPS
Per ½ cup: 74.2 Cal. / 0.01 g fat / 0% fat / 1.17 mg cholesterol

Banana fans find this ice cream very satisfying. For a total banana experience, serve scoops of banana ice cream on servings of piping hot Grilled Bananas and Rum (page 55), or on wedges of Stir-Crazy Banana-Fudge Cake (page 71).

> *4 Broiled Bananas in Their Jackets (page 56)*
> *2 cups skim milk*
> *½ cup nonfat dry milk*
> *3 tablespoons sugar*
> *1 teaspoon vanilla extract*
> *½ teaspoon ground cinnamon*
> *1 tablespoon thawed orange juice concentrate*

1. Scoop the pulp from the broiled bananas and combine with all the remaining ingredients in the container of a food processor. Process until perfectly smooth.
2. Pour into the canister of an ice cream machine and pro-

ceed according to the manufacturer's directions, or use the still-freeze method (page 109).

Brenda's Strawberry Frozen Yogurt ❋

MAKES APPROXIMATELY 2 CUPS
Per ½ cup: 106.1 Cal. / 0.0 g fat / 0% fat / 0.75 mg cholesterol

Frozen yogurt is a continuing craze. You can easily make your own version that is not overloaded with fat, excess sugar, or additives.

> 6 ounces very ripe strawberries, hulled and halved
> ⅓ cup superfine sugar
> Juice of ½ lemon
> ¾ cup nonfat yogurt
> ¼ cup puréed nonfat cottage cheese

1. Mash the berries with the sugar and lemon juice.
2. Stir together the mashed fruit and the remaining ingredients.
3. Freeze in an ice cream machine according to the manufacturer's directions, or use the still-freeze method (page 109).

Berry-Banana Frozen Yogurt

MAKES APPROXIMATELY 4¼ CUPS
Per ½ cup: 141.4 Cal. / 0.28 g fat / 2% fat / 0.33 mg cholesterol

This recipe, along with the two that follow, combines fruit (each recipe includes a ripe banana for textural richness) with nonfat yogurt and smoothed-out cottage cheese. The exact amount of sugar to use depends on the sweetness of the fruit, so always taste the mixture, and sweeten accordingly.

> *4½ cups mixed raspberries and blueberries*
> *1 very ripe banana, peeled and sliced*
> *Approximately ½ cup light brown sugar*
> *½ cup thawed orange juice concentrate*
> *1 teaspoon vanilla extract*
> *¾ cup nonfat yogurt*
> *¾ cup puréed nonfat cottage cheese*

1.   Purée berries in the blender and sieve to remove seeds.
2.   Purée the peeled banana in the blender. Add the puréed berries, the sugar, orange juice concentrate, and vanilla. Blend well. Add yogurt and cottage cheese. Pulse again a few times to blend.
3.   Freeze in the ice cream machine according to the manufacturer's directions, or use the still-freeze method (page 109). (In some machines you may have to do it in two batches.) Eat at once, or store in the freezer. After a sojourn in the freezer, the yogurt will be fairly hard. Let stand on the kitchen counter for 15 to 20 minutes before scooping.

Peach-Banana Frozen Yogurt ❋

MAKES 6 ¼ CUPS

Per ½ cup: 111.0 Cal. / 0.02 g fat / 0% fat / 0.25 mg cholesterol

> *4¼ cups (approximately 2 pounds) peeled, pitted, and cubed*
> *ripe peaches*
> *1 very ripe banana, peeled and sliced*

Approximately ½ cup light brown sugar
½ to ¾ cup thawed orange juice concentrate
1 teaspoon vanilla extract
¾ cup nonfat yogurt
¾ cup puréed nonfat cottage cheese

1. Purée the fruit in the blender.
2. Add the sugar, orange juice concentrate, and vanilla extract. Blend well. Add yogurt and cottage cheese. Pulse again a few times to blend.
3. Freeze in the ice cream machine according to the manufacturer's directions, or use the still-freeze method (page 109). (In some machines you may have to do it in two batches.) Eat at once or store in the freezer. After a sojourn in the freezer, the yogurt will be quite hard. Let stand on the kitchen counter for 15 to 20 minutes before scooping.

Pear-Banana Frozen Yogurt

MAKES 5 CUPS
Per ½ cup: 136.7 Cal. / 0.55 g fat / 4% fat / 0.30 mg cholesterol

4 cups peeled, cored, and cubed ripe pears
1 very ripe banana, peeled and sliced
Approximately ½ cup light brown sugar
¼ cup thawed orange juice concentrate
1 teaspoon vanilla extract
¾ cup nonfat yogurt
¾ cup puréed nonfat cottage cheese

1. Purée the fruit in the blender
2. Add the sugar, orange juice concentrate, and vanilla.

Blend well. Add yogurt and cottage cheese. Blend again.
3. Freeze in the ice cream machine according to the manufacturer's directions, or use the still-freeze method (page 109). (In some machines you may have to do it in two batches.) Eat at once or store in the freezer. After a sojourn in the freezer, the yogurt will be quite hard. Let stand on the kitchen counter for 15 to 20 minutes before scooping.

Chocolate Sorbet

MAKES 2½ CUPS
Per ½ cup: 295.8 Cal. / 1.62 g fat / 5% fat / 0 mg cholesterol

Chocolate sorbet tastes amazingly like good chocolate ice cream. It's hard to believe that it contains no dairy products; just water, cocoa powder, and sugar.

> *1½ cups plus 3 tablespoons granulated sugar*
> *2¼ cups water*
> *¾ cup cocoa powder, sifted*
> *½ teaspoon vanilla extract*

1. Combine the sugar and water in a saucepan and heat gently until the sugar has dissolved. Raise the heat and boil for 1 minute. Remove from the heat and allow to cool a bit.
2. In a bowl, stir a little of the sugar-water syrup into the cocoa to make a smooth paste, then gradually stir in the remaining syrup.
3. Add vanilla extract. Strain the mixture through a fine sieve.
4. Freeze in an ice cream maker following the manufacturer's instructions, or use the still-freeze method (page 109).

ICE CREAM SUNDAES

The sundae was invented in the early twentieth century because of the "blue laws," laws that determined what was allowed and what was not on Sunday. For some reason, the blue laws of the time decreed soda water inappropriate to the Sabbath. Since a favorite Sunday occupation of families in middle America was to wander over to the soda fountain for a refreshing ice cream soda, the proprietors of such establishments were in a quandary. How to satisfy their customers' cravings, without exposing them to profane soda water on the Lord's day? With ingenuity they invented a new delicacy: the ice cream soda *without* the soda. First ice cream was generously scooped into a silvery dish. Then a heavenly rich sauce was ladled over—perhaps hot fudge or chunky pineapple or crushed strawberry or marshmallow cream. Finally dollops of whipped cream were billowed on top, and a cherry crowned the whole thing. The glorious concoction was named for the day—Sunday—but the *y* was changed to an *e* so that the name of the Sabbath was not taken in vain. Thus was an enduring and beloved classic born.

Slim Cuisine Food Processor
Ice Creams ♡ 🕒

Per ½ cup peach ice cream: 23.4 Cal. / 0.03 g fat / 1% fat / 0.25 mg cholesterol
½ cup raspberry ice cream: 26.4 Cal. / 0.37 g fat / 13% fat / 0.25 mg
cholesterol

To prepare this ice cream you will need frozen berries or
frozen cubes of fruit. Buy unsweetened fruit or berries in the
store, or prepare them yourself like this: Arrange berries or
fruit cubes in one layer on nonstick baking trays and place in
the freezer. When they are solidly frozen, put the berries or
fruit cubes in plastic bags and store in the freezer until needed.
Always keep plenty of frozen fruit of all varieties in the
freezer. When you pull out a bag, if the cubes have frozen
together into one big clump, knock the bag sharply on the
kitchen counter a few times to separate.

You will also need nonfat buttermilk (see page 10), low-
Calorie sweetener, and vanilla extract.

To prepare the ice cream: Put some *still frozen* berries or fruit
cubes in the container of a food processor. How much depends on how much ice cream you want to make. Sprinkle
in just a small bit of low-Calorie sweetener, unless the fruit
is very sweet (mango, pineapple, and very ripe banana for
instance often need no added sweetener at all). Add a dash
of vanilla extract. Pour in a bit of buttermilk (¼ cup per
approximately 12 ounces of fruit). Turn on the machine.
Don't be alarmed: The machine will rattle and clatter and
vibrate all over the counter. These machines were designed
to crush ice if necessary, so you will do no damage. Let it
clatter for a minute or two. Turn off the machine, scrape
down the sides, then process again, pouring in another ¼ cup
of buttermilk. Process for another minute or two, stop and

scrape down the sides again, and taste for sweetness. Add more low-Calorie sweetener if necessary, then process until the mixture forms a smooth, beautifully creamy ice cream. You may have to stop and scrape it down another time or two; it depends on your machine. If you wish, at this point you may add some *fresh* fruit, cut into chunks, to the mixture. Pulse the machine on and off 2 or 3 times to chop the fruit and to incorporate it into the ice cream, but don't process it enough to pulverize it. The resulting fruity bits within the smooth cream are quite enchanting, especially with peach or strawberry ice cream.

As soon as this ice cream is processed, it is ready to be eaten. It can be left in the freezer for an hour, if necessary; any longer and it gets very hard. Even if you then let it stand on the counter for a while, it never regains its original glorious creaminess. So when you feel the urge, pull out the machine, grab a bag of fruit pieces from the freezer, and presto: ice cream in less than 5 minutes.

Hot Chocolate Sauce

MAKES APPROXIMATELY 2 CUPS
Per tbsp.: 9.69 Cal. / 0.04 g fat / 4% fat / 0.21 mg cholesterol

Rich, thick, and velvety, this sauce is lovely poured over chocolate or coffee ice cream for the classic "cold as winter, hot as summer" effect of a hot fudge sundae. The sauce is good cold, as well.

> 2 tablespoons cocoa powder
> 2 tablespoons cornstarch
> 1½ to 2 tablespoons sugar
> 1 tablespoon nonfat dry milk
> 1½ cups skim milk

1. Sift the dry ingredients together and combine in the blender container with the milk. Blend until perfectly smooth. Pour into an 8-cup container and cover tightly with microwave-safe plastic wrap.

2. Microwave on full power until the mixture comes to a boil (about 4 minutes). Prick the plastic wrap to release the steam, carefully remove the film, and stir the sauce with a wooden spoon.

Baked Banana-Rum-Raisin Sauce for Ice Cream ⏲♡

SERVES 1
(MAKE AS MANY PACKETS AS YOU NEED)
Per serving: 151.9 Cal. / 0 g fat / 0% fat / 0 mg cholesterol

The ingredients are baked in a hot oven in folded, crimped parchment packets. What fun when each guest, waiting with his or her portion of homemade vanilla ice cream, is handed a hot, puffy package and a pair of scissors. Snip the end of the packet and slide the contents onto the ice cream. Eat fast with a big spoon.

To enclose the bananas in parchment paper, follow the diagrams accompanying the recipe.

1 ripe banana
1 tablespoon dark rum
1 tablespoon lemon juice
1 tablespoon lime juice
1 tablespoon orange juice
Pinch of light brown sugar
½ tablespoon raisins

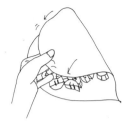

Fold a piece of parchment paper in half and cut it in the shape of a heart. Place banana chunks on one side of the heart.

Fold side opposite over the banana chunks.

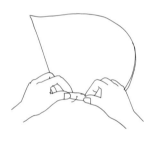

Beginning at the wide end of the heart and working toward the tapered end, fold over a section of paper about 2 inches long with your fingers, so as to seal the edges together, and pinch firmly. As you work, leave space on top so that the paper does not touch the fruit.

After making the first pinch, fold over the next 2-inch section of paper, overlapping the first fold and pinch slightly, and pinch it together, and so on, all around the open edge of the heart until the packet is sealed. The last fold on the tapered end can be twisted to secure the packet. Make sure that all edges are folded together and crimped by the pinching movement.

1. Preheat oven to 425° F.
2. Cut bananas in half lengthwise, then cut crosswise into ½ inch chunks. Place on parchment paper heart.
3. Evenly sprinkle all remaining ingredients over the banana. Follow the instructions accompanying the step-by-step illustrations for enclosing the banana chunks in parchment paper.
4. Put the packet on a baking sheet and bake for 10 minutes. The packet will become browned and puffy.
5. Serve each diner a hot, puffy packet, a pair of scissors, and a portion of Vanilla Ice Cream (page 109).

♡ Omit sugar and raisins.

Fruit Coulis

Raspberry (per 12 ounces): 166.6 Cal. / 2.73 g fat / 15% fat / 0 mg cholesterol
Strawberry (per 12 ounces): 101.5 Cal. / 0 g fat / 0% fat / 0 mg cholesterol

This method works beautifully with fresh or frozen and thawed fruits and berries. Try mango, peaches, raspberries, blueberries, strawberries, huckleberries, black currants, or blackberries. Strawberry coulis is particularly delicious with Chocolate Sorbet (page 118).

Purée the peeled, pitted ripe fruit or berries in the processor or blender. If the fruit or berries are particularly fibrous or the berries contain seeds, sieve the purée. Sweeten to taste with granulated sugar substitute. If the taste needs sharpening, squeeze in just a bit of lemon juice. Refrigerate until needed.

FRUIT RICKEYS ⏲

Old-fashioned soda fountains sold fruit rickeys in addition to milkshakes and ice cream
sodas, but most kids weren't interested—they
preferred the over-the-top cream-laden ex-
cesses of the shakes and sodas to the tart re-
freshment of the rickeys. But for an adult (and
for discerning children) a fruit rickey is a wonderful treat. To make one, pour some Fruit
Coulis (page 124) or some citrus juice (orange
juice or sweetened lemon or lime juice) into
the bottom of a tall, chilled glass. Pour in very
cold sparkling water, stirring all the while with
a long-handled spoon. Press a generous scoop
of Fruit Sorbet (pages 134–39) onto the rim of
the glass. Provide a long straw and a long-
handled spoon. This is the perfect tall, cold
drink to enjoy on a hot summer's day.

♡ Sweeten the citrus juice with granulated
sugar substitute.

Vanilla Milkshake ♡

M AKES APPROXIMATELY 7 ½ CUPS
Per cup: 43.18 Cal. / 0 g fat / 0% fat / 2.07 mg cholesterol

In smaller quantities this vanilla shake can be used as a
whipped cream–type topping for ice cream sundaes, ice cream

sodas, and any desserts that would benefit from a creamy dollop or two. (If you are preparing it as whipped cream, rather than a shake, halve or quarter the recipe.)

2½ cups skim milk slush (see Note)
6 tablespoons nonfat dry milk
2 tablespoons vanilla granulated sugar substitute (page 8)

1.   Combine about ¾ of the milk slush and the remaining ingredients in a food processor.
2.   Process until thick (the consistency of whipped cream), and greatly increased in bulk (at *least* 2 minutes of processing). The longer you process the mixture, the stiffer and more like whipped cream it becomes. Add the rest of the slush gradually, as it processes. Pour into cold glasses and serve at once, with spoons, or use as whipped "cream" for berries, bananas, and the like.

I I I I VARIATIONS I I I I   ♡

Coffee: Follow recipe for vanilla, but use ¾ the amount of milk slush and add ½ cup coffee slush (see Note).
Mocha: Make the vanilla milkshake. When the mixture has become very thick, add, while the mixture is processing, ½ to 1 teaspoon instant espresso granules. When everything is thoroughly amalgamated, taste and process in a bit more sweetener if necessary. Serve at once.

NOTE: To make skim milk slush, freeze 2½ cups of skim milk in a cardboard milk carton. When you want to make a milkshake, remove the carton from the freezer and, with scissors, cut off the top, and cut the carton away from the frozen block of milk. Put the milk into a microwave receptacle and microwave on high for 2 or 3 minutes, until slushy and partially melted. With a spoon or a dull knife chop and mush up the milk until the texture is consistently slushy.

If you do not have a microwave, freeze the milk in its carton until it is partially frozen and slushy. Proceed with the recipe.

To make coffee slush: store strong filter coffee in the freezer. Defrost in the microwave until slushy.

Strawberry Cream ♡

MAKES APPROXIMATELY 8 CUPS
Per cup: 37.05 Cal. / 0 g fat / 0% fat / 0.91 mg cholesterol

The milkshake/whipped cream technique can be used to create outstanding fruit mousses. You might call this the thinking person's junk food. It's great for people who love to overeat sweet creamy things, but hate the resulting flab.

> *1¼ cups skim milk slush (see Note, page 126)*
> *3 tablespoons nonfat dry milk*
> *½ teaspoon orange extract*
> *½ teaspoon vanilla extract*
> *1 pound hulled, quartered, very ripe strawberries*
> *Granulated sugar substitute to taste*

1. Combine the milk slush, dry milk, orange extract, and vanilla in a food processor and process until the mixture is as thick as softly whipped cream and greatly increased in bulk.
2. While the machine is running, drop the strawberries through the feed tube, a handful at a time. When all are added, stop and taste. Add sweetener to taste, then continue processing for another minute or so, until the mixture is so thick that a spoon inserted in it will stand straight up. The mixture will have expanded to fill the entire processor container. Serve and eat at once.

Chocolate Milkshake

MAKES 7 ½ CUPS
Per cup: 49.34 Cal. / 0.19 g fat / 4% fat / 2.07 mg cholesterol

2½ cups skim milk slush (see Note, page 126)
6 tablespoons nonfat dry milk
3 tablespoons vanilla granulated sugar substitute (page 8)
2 or 3 heaping tablespoons sifted cocoa powder

1.   Combine ¾ of the milk slush and all the remaining ingredients in a food processor.
2.   Process until thick (the consistency of whipped cream), and greatly increased in bulk (at *least* 2 minutes of processing). The longer you process the mixture, the stiffer and more like whipped cream it becomes. Add the rest of the slush gradually as it processes. Pour into cold glasses and serve at once, with spoons.

Vanilla Fruit Parfaits

MAKES 8 CUPS
Per cup: 44.7 Cal. / 0.11 g fat / 2% fat / 1.81 mg cholesterol

Half vanilla "whipped" cream and half fruit mousse make a festive dessert.

2½ cups skim milk slush (see Note, page 126)
6 tablespoons nonfat dry milk
1 teaspoon vanilla extract

Granulated sugar substitute to taste
4 to 6 ounces cubes of frozen fruit or berries (see pages
  120–21)

1.   Put the milk slush, dry milk, vanilla, and granulated sugar substitute in a food processor. Process for at *least* 2 minutes, until mixture is the consistency of whipped cream and has greatly increased in volume. Stop the machine. Divide half of the mixture among large clear glass dessert goblets.
2.   Turn the machine back on. As it processes, add the fruit, a few pieces at a time. Stop and push the pieces of fruit down onto the blades. Taste and add a little more sweetener if necessary. Continue processing until the mixture is smooth, thick, and all the fruit is blended together. Spoon an equal amount of the fruit cream on each portion of the vanilla cream. Serve at once.

Black and White Parfaits   ♡

M A K E S   7 ½   C U P S
Per cup: 56.6 Cal. / 0.13 g fat / 2% fat / 1.93 mg cholesterol

2½ cups skim milk slush (see Note, page 126)
6 tablespoons nonfat dry milk
1 to 2 teaspoons vanilla extract
Granulated sugar substitute to taste
1½ tablespoons cocoa powder, sifted

1.   Put the milk slush, dry milk, vanilla, and sweetener to taste in a food processor. Process for at *least* 2 minutes, until mixture is the consistency of whipped cream and has greatly increased in volume. Stop the machine. Divide half of the

mixture among large clear glass dessert goblets.

2. Turn the machine back on. While it is running, sprinkle the cocoa powder into the mixture through the feed tube. Stop the machine and add more sweetener to taste. Process for another minute or so. Spoon an equal amount of chocolate mixture on each portion of the vanilla mixture. Serve at once.

BANANA SPLITS

What's the ultimate ice cream fantasy? The banana split, of course. Bananas are the healthy eater's best friend: no fat, bursting with vitamins, minerals, and lovely complex carbohydrate—a perfectly packaged, sweet and friendly, always accessible fruit. Split the exemplary fruit and smother it in Slim Cuisine ice creams and sorbets: vanilla, chocolate, mango, raspberry, strawberry, peach, pear, pineapple, whatever pleases you. Why not a little of each?

Blanket the bananas and their lavish ice creams and sorbets with Hot Chocolate Sauce (page 121), Raspberry Coulis (page 124), and—instead of high-fat chopped nuts—sprinkle the whole thing with crumbled amaretti cookies and crunchy toasted wheat cereal. Now *that's* a banana split!

♡ To make a wonderful banana split that conforms to the Slim Cuisine weight-*loss* regime, use fruit coulis only (no hot fudge sauce) and Slim Cuisine food processor ice creams sweetened with granulated sugar substitute. Sprinkle the top of the banana split with crunchy toasted wheat cereal.

Cold Blueberry Soup

MAKES APPROXIMATELY 3 CUPS

Per ½ cup: 82.9 Cal. / 0 g fat / 0% fat / 0 mg cholesterol

This cold soup is meant to be served as dessert, with a scoop of Blueberry Sorbet (recipe follows) centered in each bowlful. The soup with its sorbet is visually stunning, and usually brings gasps of delight from dinner guests.

> 1 pound blueberries
> Approximately 1¾ cups water
> 1 small lemon, sliced and seeded
> 1 cinnamon stick
> ⅓ cup vanilla sugar (see page 8)

1.   Combine berries, water, lemon, cinnamon, and sugar in a nonreactive saucepan. Bring to a boil, reduce heat, and simmer for 10 minutes. Cool.
2.   Remove the lemon slices and cinnamon stick. Purée the soup in the blender until very smooth and velvety. Pour into a jar and chill. Shake well before serving.
3.   To serve, pour chilled soup into shallow soup plates. Put a scoop of sorbet in the center of each serving.

| | | | VARIATION | | | |

Per ½ cup: 42.9 Cal. / 0 g fat / 0% fat / 0 mg cholesterol

♡   Omit sugar. Sweeten to taste with granulated sugar substitute after the soup has cooled.

Blueberry Sorbet ♡ ⏱

MAKES 3 ¾ CUPS SORBET
Per ½ cup: 36.57 Cal. / 0 g fat / 0% fat / 0 mg cholesterol

If you use the Slim Cuisine Food Processor Ice Cream method (page 120) but substitute unsweetened fruit juice for the buttermilk, the result is a beautiful instant sorbet. As with the ice creams, they may be eaten at once, or stored in the freezer for up to 1 hour.

> *12 ounces frozen blueberries (see page 120 for the method*
> *for freezing berries)*
> *1 teaspoon vanilla extract*
> *Approximately ½ cup unsweetened apple juice*
> *Granulated sugar substitute to taste*

1.   Combine berries and vanilla in the food processor container. Pour in ¼ cup apple juice.
2.   Process until berries are roughly chopped. Taste and add a bit of granulated sugar substitute if necessary. Continue processing. Pour in the remaining juice as it processes. Stop and scrape down the container as needed. When the mixture forms a smooth sorbet consistency, serve at once, or scrape into a container and freeze for up to 1 hour.

Peach-Raspberry Soup

MAKES APPROXIMATELY 3 CUPS
Per ½ cup: 129.5 Cal. / 0.57 g fat / 4% fat / 0 mg cholesterol

This soup and its companion Peach Sorbet (recipe follows) are made with pantry staples. Although both are made with canned fruit, there is absolutely no compromise of taste in the finished dish.

One 15-ounce can sliced peaches in natural juice
One 15-ounce can raspberries in natural juice
¼ cup sugar
1 tablespoon orange liqueur (Cointreau or Grand Marnier)
1 cup sweet white wine
1 teaspoon vanilla extract
1 cinnamon stick
Slivered zest of ½ small lemon
Slivered zest of ½ small orange
1 slice lemon, seeded

1.   Combine the fruits and their juices with all remaining ingredients in a nonreactive saucepan. Bring to a boil, then reduce heat and simmer for 10 minutes. Cool.
2.   Remove lemon slice and cinnamon stick. Purée the soup in the blender or processor until very smooth, then push through a sieve. Pour into a jar and chill. Shake well before serving.
3.   Pour soup into beautiful shallow soup plates. Place a generous dollop of Peach Sorbet in the center of each portion, and garnish with mint leaves if you like.

▌▌▌▌ VARIATION ▌▌▌▌

Per ½ cup: 99.5 Cal. / 0.57 g fat / 5% fat / 0 mg cholesterol

♡ Omit sugar. Sweeten to taste with granulated sugar substitute after the soup has cooled.

Peach Sorbet

MAKES 2½ CUPS
Per ½ cup: 36.76 Cal. / 0 g fat / 0% fat / 0 mg cholesterol

If the peach slices are frozen in advance, this recipe—as with all Slim Cuisine food processor ice creams and sorbets—takes scant minutes to make.

> *One 15-ounce can sliced peaches in natural juice*
> *½ teaspoon vanilla extract*
> *Granulated sugar substitute as needed*
> *A few drops of fresh lemon juice*

1.   Drain peaches *very* well, saving the juice. Refrigerate the juices. Spread the drained peach slices out on a nonstick tray and freeze. When they are thoroughly frozen, put into a plastic bag and store in the freezer until needed.
2.   Put the frozen peach slices in the container of the processor, along with the vanilla and ¼ cup peach juice. Process for a minute or so. Stop and scrape down the container. Turn the machine on again and process, gradually adding another ¼ cup peach juice and a few drops of lemon juice as it processes. Stop, scrape down, and taste. Add a bit of granulated sugar substitute and a bit more lemon juice as needed. Process until very smooth and fluffy. Serve at once, or scrape into a container and store in the freezer for up to an hour.

Hot and Cold Pineapple

MAKES 2 CUPS
Per ½ cup: 91.85 Cal. / 0.72 g fat / 7% fat / 0 mg cholesterol

Another "hot as summer, cold as winter" extravaganza; this time, cubes of hot, rum-soaked pineapple, topped with scoops of juicy, freshly made Pineapple Sorbet (recipe follows).

> 1 large ripe pineapple, peeled and cored
> 1½ to 3 tablespoons light brown sugar (depending on sweetness of the pineapple)
> ¼ cup dark rum
> Pineapple Sorbet

1. Preheat the oven to 400° F.
2. Cut the peeled, cored pineapple into 1-inch pieces. Put them in a shallow nonreactive baking dish.
3. Combine the sugar and rum in a saucepan. Bring to a boil, stirring occasionally. Boil for 1 minute. Pour the mixture over the pineapple and stir to combine. Cover and bake for 40 minutes.
4. Divide the hot pineapple among 4 goblets. Pour the hot juices over the pineapple. Top each with a generous scoop of cold sorbet.

❙❙❙❙ VARIATION ❙❙❙❙

Per ½ cup: 72.61 Cal. / 0.72 g fat / 9% fat / 0 mg cholesterol

♡ Omit sugar.

Pineapple Sorbet

MAKES 2 CUPS
Per ½ cup: 58.85 Cal. / 0.45 g fat / 7% fat / 0 mg cholesterol

This sorbet is *pure pineapple*. See page 120 for preparing and storing the frozen pineapple cubes. If the pineapple is tart, you may want to sweeten the sorbet with a bit of granulated sugar substitute, but a truly ripe pineapple is usually sweet enough.

> *1 cup (10 ounces) frozen pineapple cubes*
> *1 tablespoon vanilla extract*
> *1 tablespoon dark rum*
> *Approximately ¼ cup unsweetened pineapple juice*

1.   Combine pineapple, vanilla, rum, and ⅛ cup juice in the processor container. Process until roughly chopped. Stop and scrape down the container.
2.   Begin processing again. As mixture processes, pour in the remaining juice. When the mixture forms a sorbet consistency (you may have to stop and scrape it down another time or two), scrape into a container and store in the freezer for up to an hour.

Banana-Ginger Sorbet

MAKES APPROXIMATELY 2 CUPS
Per ½ cup: 78.32 Cal. / 0 g fat / 0% fat / 0 mg cholesterol

I have to call this a sorbet because it contains *no* dairy products at all, but it is really rich and creamy enough to be called an ice cream. Try this sorbet on Grilled Bananas and Rum (page 55). The sensation of eating the hot, tender bananas in their caramelized juices sizzling under a scoop of this creamy, rich, slowly melting cold sorbet is indescribable.

1¾ cups (10 ounces) frozen banana slices (see page 120)
1 lump crystallized ginger, diced (use scissors)
Juice of 1 orange
½ teaspoon vanilla extract

1.   Place the frozen banana slices in the container of the food processor. Add the ginger, orange juice, and vanilla extract.
2.   Turn on the processor and let it run until the mixture is beautifully smooth and creamy. Stop and scrape down the sides if necessary. Serve at once or scrape into a container and freeze for up to an hour.

Orange-Buttermilk Sherbet

MAKES APPROXIMATELY 2 CUPS
Per ½ cup: 144.4 Cal. / 0.12 g fat / 1% fat / 1.25 mg cholesterol

This recipe is based on a remembered childhood treat from the white-uniformed ice cream vendor who pedaled his cart down neighborhood streets, ringing his little bell. His orange creamsicle was vanilla ice cream encased in orange sherbet and impaled on a stick. Ever since, I've loved that combination of flavors. This is an adult version, much tarter than what I remember from forty years ago, but it successfully combines vanilla creaminess with orange iciness.

2½ cups fresh orange juice
4 to 5 tablespoons sugar
Granulated sugar substitute to taste
1 teaspoon vanilla extract
½ teaspoon slivered orange zest
Approximately 1¼ cups buttermilk

1.   Combine all ingredients in the blender. Blend until very smooth.

2.   Freeze in an ice cream maker according to the manufacturer's directions. Store in the freezer. Serve in scoops, as you would sorbet or ice cream.

I I I I   VARIATIONS   I I I I

❄ *Grapefruit-Buttermilk Sherbet:* Prepare as for orange-buttermilk sherbet, but substitute grapefruit juice concentrate for orange juice. You will probably need to add more sweetener.

Melon Sorbet   ❄

MAKES 2 ½ CUPS
Per ½ cup: 61.4 Cal. / 0.28 g fat / 4% fat / 0 mg cholesterol

An icy and refreshing essence of summer. Serve in melon halves or frozen in hollowed-out orange shells. Or serve in a goblet of apple/raspberry juice.

   1¾ cups seedless cubes honeydew melon, with juices
   1¾ cups seedless cubes watermelon, with juices
   1 tablespoon orange liqueur (Cointreau or Grand Marnier)

1½ to 2 tablespoons sugar
Apple juice (if necessary)
Approximately 1 teaspoon fresh lime juice

1.   Combine the melon cubes, their juices, the orange liqueur, and the sugar in a nonreactive bowl. Mash together with a potato masher. Pour the mixture into a 1-quart measuring cup. If necessary, add apple juice so the mixture measures 2½ cups. Process in the blender to a rough purée. Add lime juice (exact amount depends on the sweetness of the melons).

2.   Process in an electric ice cream maker according to the manufacturer's directions.

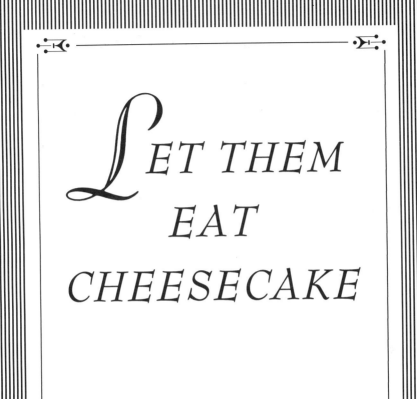

*L*ET THEM
EAT
CHEESECAKE

When I think about cheesecake, I think about extravagant creaminess in a crumb crust. I have switched from a butter-bound crust to an egg-white bound one, and the crumbs I use are now low-fat ones.

But it is in the filling itself that I have completely broken with tradition. Instead of the classic killer combo of egg yolks, creams, and cream cheese, use a whipped ricotta mixture (or quark if you can find it—see page 10). Another departure: Classic cheesecakes are baked; mine are not.

Forget the killer cheesecakes—satisfy your cheesecake longings with these lovely, low-fat cheese pies.

CRUMB CRUSTS

Choose the crust you want for your cheesecake: Grape-Nuts, amaretti (almond flavor), or half-and-half.

PLAIN CRUMB CRUST

Preheat the oven to 350° F. Put 1¼ cups of Grape-Nuts into the blender or processor and process to coarse crumbs, or put cereal in a plastic bag and reduce it to coarse crumbs with a rolling pin. Lightly beat 2 egg whites. With two spoons, toss together the cereal crumbs and the egg white until the former is thoroughly coated with the latter. Lightly spray a 10-inch round nonstick pie pan with vegetable spray. Scrape the crumb mixture into the pan. With the back of a serving spoon, spread the crumbs evenly over the bottom and up the sides to form a thin layer. Bake 5 to 7 minutes. Cool. When crust is cool, spread and swirl the cheesecake mixture over it. Chill for several hours or overnight. During the chilling process, the crust will soften to just the right consistency.

AMARETTI CRUMB CRUST

Preheat the oven to 350° F. Put 1 cup of amaretti cookies into the blender or processor. Process to coarse crumbs. Or put cookies in a plastic bag and reduce them to coarse crumbs with a rolling pin. Lightly beat 1 egg white. In a bowl, toss the crumbs and egg white together until the former is thoroughly coated with the latter. Lightly spray a 10-inch round nonstick pie pan with vegetable spray. Scrape the crumb mixture into the pan. With the back of a serving spoon spread it evenly over the bottom and up the sides. Bake 7 to 10 minutes. Cool on a rack.

HALF-AND-HALF CRUMB CRUST

Make the crust as above, but use ½ cup amaretti cookies, ½ cup Grape-Nuts, and 2 egg whites.

Rum Raisin Cheese Pie

SERVES 8   MAKES ONE 10-INCH PIE

Per serving
  (using ricotta): 174.1 Cal. / 3.50 g fat / 18% fat / 14.00 mg cholesterol
  (using quark): 154.7 Cal. / 0 g fat / 0% fat / 0 mg cholesterol

In this cheese pie, and a few of the ones that follow, sweetness is provided by pulverized raisins or currants and a bit of granulated sugar substitute. Sweetness is very much a matter of taste; you must taste the mixture and adjust the amount of sweetener to your liking.

> *6 generous tablespoons raisins*
> *¼ cup dark rum*
> *1 teaspoon vanilla extract*
> *5 tablespoons water*
> *Finely slivered zest of 1 small orange*
> *Finely slivered zest of 1 small lemon*
> *28 ounces low-fat ricotta cheese or quark*
> *Granulated sugar substitute to taste*
> *Half-and-Half Crumb Crust (above)*

GARNISH

> *1 teaspoon light brown sugar*
> *½ tablespoon Grape-Nuts*

1.   Combine raisins, rum, vanilla, water, and zests. Simmer until raisins are plump and liquid has reduced to ½ tablespoon. Cool.

2.   Combine the raisin mixture and the ricotta cheese or quark in the processor container. Process for a moment or so. Taste, and sweeten as needed with sugar substitute. Process until fluffy. By the time you have finished processing, the raisins will be puréed. Scrape the mixture into a cheese-cloth-lined sieve over a bowl and refrigerate for a few hours or overnight.

3.   Spread and swirl the mixture into the crust.

4.   To make the crumb topping mix the brown sugar and the cereal. Sprinkle garnish lightly over the pie. Chill.

Amaretti Cheese Pie

S E R V E S   8   M A K E S   O N E   1 0 - I N C H   P I E

Per serving
  (using ricotta): 167.9 Cal. / 3.50 g fat / 19% fat / 14.00 mg cholesterol
  (using quark): 148.4 Cal. / 0 g fat / 0% fat / 0 mg cholesterol

This is one of the most elegant cheese pies in the collection; very appropriate for special occasions.

   6 generous tablespoons raisins
   1 teaspoon vanilla extract
   1½ teaspoons almond extract
   ½ cup water
   28 ounces low-fat ricotta cheese or quark
   Approximately 1 tablespoon granulated sugar substitute
   A few drops of lemon juice
   Amaretti Crumb Crust (page 144)
   2 pairs amaretti cookies, for garnish

1. Combine raisins, vanilla, 1 teaspoon almond extract, and water in a small frying pan. Simmer until the raisins are plump and the liquid has reduced to ½ to 1 tablespoon. Cool thoroughly.

2. Combine the raisin mixture and the ricotta or quark in the processor container. Process for a moment or so. Taste and sweeten as needed with granulated sugar substitute (½ to 1 tablespoon). Sprinkle in the lemon juice and the remaining ½ teaspoon almond extract. Process until mixture is fluffy and the raisins are puréed. Scrape the mixture into a cheesecloth-lined sieve over a bowl and refrigerate for a few hours or overnight.

3. Spread and swirl the mixture over the amaretti crust. With a kitchen mallet, crush the amaretti cookies and sprinkle the crumbs evenly over the cheese layer. Chill.

Pineapple Cheese Pie

SERVES 8   MAKES ONE 10-INCH PIE

Per serving: 196.8 Cal. / 0 g fat / 0% fat / 0.09 mg cholesterol

Canned crushed pineapple beaten into ricotta makes one of the most pleasing cheese pies of all. The filling can also be used to make a Coeur à la Crème (page 151).

> *30 ounces (1½ cans) crushed pineapple in natural juice*
> *28 ounces low-fat ricotta cheese or quark*
> *1 teaspoon vanilla extract*
> *Approximately 2 tablespoons granulated sugar substitute*
> *Half-and-Half Crumb Crust (page 145)*

GARNISH

½ tablespoon Grape-Nuts
½ amaretti cookie
1 teaspoon light brown sugar

1.   Drain the pineapple in a sieve set over a bowl. Press down on the pineapple pulp to extract as much juice as possible. (Save the juice for another use.)
2.   Combine *half* the pineapple with the ricotta or quark and the vanilla in the container of the food processor. Process until very smooth and fluffy. Add granulated sugar substitute to taste, and process until blended.
3.   Gently fold in the remaining pineapple with a rubber spatula.
4.   Line a sieve with cheesecloth and place it over a deep bowl. Scrape the cheese mixture into the sieve. Refrigerate and allow to drain overnight.
5.   When the cheese mixture is firm and well drained, swirl and spread it into the crust.
6.   Reduce the Grape-Nuts and the amaretti cookie to crumbs in the food processor. Stir in the brown sugar. Sprinkle this garnish evenly over the cheese layer. Chill.

IIII VARIATION **IIII**

Pineapple Cheese Pie for Weight Loss
Per serving: 173 Cal. / 0 g fat / 0% fat / 0 mg cholesterol
♡   Use quark instead of ricotta. Omit the topping, and use a Plain Crumb crust (page 144).

Mandarin-Ginger Cheese Pie

SERVES 8   MAKES ONE 10-INCH PIE

Per serving
  (using ricotta): 194.2 Cal. / 3.50 g fat / 16% fat / 14.0 mg cholesterol
  (using quark): 174.8 Cal. / 0 g fat / 0% fat / 0 mg cholesterol

I love the bracing gingery bite of this cheese pie, but if you are not a ginger fan, leave out the crystallized ginger, and enjoy the orange flavor on its own.

> *Two 11-ounce cans mandarin oranges in natural juice*
> *28 ounces low-fat ricotta cheese or quark*
> *1 teaspoon vanilla extract*
> *1 generous teaspoon (½ ounce) crystallized ginger*
> *1 tablespoon orange liqueur or orange juice from mandarins*
> *A few drops of lemon juice*
> *Granulated sugar substitute to taste*
> *Half-and-Half Crumb Crust (page 145)*
> *Mandarin orange slices*
> *Crystallized ginger slivers*

1. Drain the mandarin oranges in a sieve set over a bowl. Press down on the mandarin pulp to extract as much juice as possible. (Save the extra juice for another use.)
2. Combine *half* the mandarins with the ricotta or quark, vanilla, crystallized ginger, orange liqueur or juice, and lemon juice in the container of a food processor. Process until very smooth and fluffy. Add granulated sugar substitute to taste, and process until blended.
3. Gently fold in the remaining mandarins with a rubber spatula.
4. Line a sieve with cheesecloth or a jelly bag, and place it over a deep bowl. Scrape the cheese mixture into the sieve. Refrigerate and allow to drain overnight.

||||||||||||||||||||||||||||||||||||||||||||||||||||||||||||||||||||||||||||||||

5. When the cheese mixture is firm and well drained, swirl and spread it into the crust. Chill. Garnish with additional drained, blotted dry mandarin slices and slivers of diced crystallized ginger.

Chocolate Cheese Pie

SERVES 8 TO 10
MAKES ONE 10-INCH CHEESE PIE

Per serving:
(⅛, using ricotta): 223.2 Cal. / 4.24 g fat / 17% fat / 14.28 mg cholesterol
(¹/₁₀, using ricotta): 178.6 Cal. / 3.39 g fat / 17% fat / 11.42 mg cholesterol
(⅛, using quark): 203.7 Cal. / 0.74 g fat / 3% fat / 0.28 mg cholesterol
(¹/₁₀, using quark): 163.0 Cal. / 0.59 g fat / 3% fat / 0.22 mg cholesterol

A chocolate encounter of the intense kind, for those who consider chocolate an essential nutrient.

1 recipe Hot Buttermilk Fudge Sauce, cooled (page 170)
28 ounces low-fat ricotta cheese or quark
Plain Crumb Crust (page 144)

1. Combine the sauce and the ricotta or quark in the food processor or blender. Process until very smooth and fluffy. Line a sieve with cheesecloth and place over a deep bowl. Scrape the chocolate mixture into the sieve. Refrigerate overnight to drain.
2. Swirl and spread the chocolate filling over the crust. Chill.

COEUR À LA CRÈME

Coeur à la crème molds are small, pierced, heart-shaped molds made of white porcelain. They are available in many cookware shops. Coeurs à la crème are made by lining the mold with cheesecloth that has been rinsed in cold water and wrung out, then spooning a creamy mixture into the lined molds. The overhanging cheesecoth is flipped over to cover the mixture and the molds are set on a plate to drain in the refrigerator for several hours or overnight. At serving time, coat each small plate with a fruit coulis (page 124), unwrap the mold, and flip the drained, heart-shaped creamy mixture onto the coulis. Garnish with berries or mint leaves if you wish. Any of the cheesecake fillings (pages 145–50) or tiramisù toppings (pages 152–55) would make splendid coeurs à la crème. Large molds are available as well if you prefer to make one large one instead of individual servings.

Tiramisù

SERVES 8

FILLS A 12-BY-7-INCH BAKING DISH

Per serving

  (using lady fingers): 151.3 Cal. / 3.18 g fat / 19% fat / 6.09 mg cholesterol

  (using bread base): 118.68 Cal. / 1.58 g fat / 12% fat / 6.09 mg cholesterol

  (using angel sheet cake base): 246.5 Cal. / 1.68 g fat / 6% fat /

    6.09 mg cholesterol

Tiramisù seems to be everyone's favorite dessert. It is so familiar that one feels as if it were a traditional recipe, but it is only 15 to 20 years old, and not characteristic of any particular region of Italy. It's simply made of Italian ladyfingers and mascarpone cheese (sometimes the mascarpone is mixed with heavy cream and/or egg yolks). The whole thing is then topped with grated chocolate. Slim Cuisine tiramisù uses the same ladyfingers (or replaces them with bread or angel cake fingers, see variations), but it substitutes low-fat ricotta (or ricotta mixed with nonfat cottage cheese or quark to bring the fat down even further) for the mascarpone, it cuts down on the sugar, and it uses cocoa powder in place of grated chocolate. Just try it and you'll agree that Slim Cuisine does not compromise on flavor.

> *15 to 16 Italian ladyfingers (see Notes)*
> *½ cup strong black coffee (see Notes)*
> *1 tablespoon Amaretto di Saronno or dark rum*
> *1 tablespoon brandy*
> *¾ pound low-fat ricotta cheese*
> *¾ pound nonfat cottage cheese or quark*
> *3 or 4 tablespoons granulated sugar substitute*
> *1½ teaspoons vanilla extract*
> *1 heaped tablespoon cocoa powder*
> *1½ teaspoons confectioners' sugar*

1. Line the bottom of a shallow rectangular or oval baking dish with a layer of the ladyfingers. Stir together the coffee, Amaretto di Saronno or rum, and brandy. A tablespoon at a time, sprinkle this mixture over the ladyfingers. They should be well moistened but not soggy.

2. Combine the ricotta cheese, cottage cheese or quark, granulated sugar substitute, and 1½ teaspoons vanilla in the food processor. Process until smooth and fluffy. Spread this mixture smoothly over the ladyfingers.

3. Combine the cocoa and confectioners' sugar. Sift evenly over surface of the dessert. Cover the dish and chill.

NOTES: Ladyfingers are *low*-fat, but not *no*-fat; they are made with whole eggs. If you must (or you cook for someone who must) avoid fat and cholesterol altogether, see the variations below.

In this recipe and the following one, water process decaffeinated filter coffee can be substituted for the strong coffee with absolutely no loss of quality. If you are planning to serve tiramisù to children, substitute fruit juice for the liqueurs.

IIII VARIATIONS IIII

Bread Base: Instead of ladyfingers use 3 or 4 slices of nonfat or low-fat bakery white bread, ¾ inch thick, trimmed of crusts and cut into fingers 1 inch wide. Decrease the amount of coffee to 1 to 2 tablespoons. Any of the fillings may be used with this base.

Angel Sheet Cake Base: Use the Chocolate or plain Angel Sheet Cake (pages 67–70). Cut the cake into 1-inch fingers. Decrease the amount of coffee to 3 tablespoons.

Orange-Ricotta: Use 28 ounces low-fat ricotta cheese blended with 1 heaped tablespoon orange marmalade, granulated sugar substitute to taste, 1 teaspoon vanilla extract, and 1 tablespoon orange liqueur (Grand Marnier or Cointreau). Spread this mixture over one of the Tiramisù bases. Sprinkle with cocoa and confectioners' sugar as described in main recipe.

Meringue: Use 1 pound low-fat ricotta cheese blended with 1½ teaspoons vanilla extract. Beat 2 (room temperature) egg whites with a pinch of cream of tartar until they hold soft peaks. A little at a time beat in 2 or 3 tablespoons superfine sugar. Beat until the sugar is dissolved, and the egg whites are glossy and hold firm peaks. Stir 2 generous tablespoons of the egg whites into the ricotta to lighten it. Fold the rest of the egg whites into the mixture with a rubber spatula, using an over and under motion, and turn the bowl as you fold. Spread this mixture over one of the Tiramisù bases. Sprinkle with cocoa and confectioners' sugar as described in main recipe. This is a particularly delicious version of tiramisù, but because raw egg white is used in this variation, use only the freshest eggs from a trusted supplier. And it is *never* a good idea to feed a raw egg dish to a child, a pregnant woman, an elderly person, or to someone who is medically compromised.

Chocolate Tiramisù

SERVES 8

FILLS A 12-BY-7-INCH BAKING DISH

Per serving

(using ladyfingers): 175.0 Cal. / 3.35 g fat / 17% fat / 6.09 mg cholesterol

(using bread base): 143.8 Cal. / 2.25 g fat / 14% fat / 6.59 mg cholesterol

(using angel sheet cake base): 270.1 Cal / 1.85 g fat / 6% fat / 6.09 mg cholesterol

Beat cocoa powder into the ricotta layer, and sprinkle it on top, and you have chocolate tiramisù, to gladden the hearts

of chocolate connoisseurs everywhere. It tastes rich and chocolatey, yet the fat levels have been drastically reduced.

> *15 or 16 Italian ladyfingers (see Note, page 153)*
> *½ cup strong black coffee (see Note, page 153)*
> *1 tablespoon Amaretto di Saronno, or ½ teaspoon
>   almond extract*
> *1 tablespoon dark rum*
> *¾ pound low-fat ricotta cheese*
> *¾ pound nonfat cottage cheese*
> *6½ tablespoons confectioners' sugar*
> *3 generous tablespoons cocoa powder*
> *1½ teaspoons vanilla extract*

1.   Line the bottom of a shallow rectangular or oval baking
dish with one layer of ladyfingers. Stir together the coffee,
Amaretto di Saronno, and rum. A tablespoon at a time,
sprinkle this mixture over the sponge fingers.
2.   Combine the ricotta and cottage cheese, 6 tablespoons of
the confectioners' sugar, 2 tablespoons cocoa, and 1½ teaspoons vanilla in the food processor. Process until smooth
and fluffy. Spread this mixture smoothly over the ladyfingers.
3.   Sift together the remaining heaping tablespoon cocoa and
½ tablespoon confectioners' sugar. Sprinkle evenly over the
surface of the dessert. Cover the dish and chill.

Fruit Ricotta Extravaganza

S E R V E S   8
F I L L S   A   1 2 - B Y - 7 - I N C H   B A K I N G   D I S H
Per serving: 172.9 Cal. / 4.34 g fat / 23% fat / 11.00 mg cholesterol

This is a tiramisù with a layer of fresh summer fruit nestled
between the ladyfingers and the topping.

15 to 16 Italian sponge fingers (see Note)
8 ounces strawberries
8 ounces blueberries
8 ounces raspberries
2 ripe peaches
1 teaspoon vanilla extract
2 tablespoons fresh orange juice
1 tablespoon orange liqueur (Grand Marnier or Cointreau)
22 ounces low-fat ricotta cheese
3 tablespoons confectioners' sugar
2 pairs amaretti cookies

1.   Line the bottom of a shallow rectangular or oval clear glass baking dish with a layer of sponge fingers (you may have to break a few in half).
2.   Halve or quarter the strawberries. Combine all the berries in a bowl. Peel, halve, and pit the peaches and cut them into cubes. Add to the berries. Sprinkle on ½ teaspoon vanilla and all the orange juice and liqueur and gently toss with two spoons to combine thoroughly. Spread fruit mixture and juices all over the sponge fingers.
3.   Put the ricotta cheese into a food processor with the remaining ½ teaspoon vanilla and the sugar. Process until smooth and fluffy and perfectly amalgamated.
4.   With a rubber spatula, smooth and spread the cheese mixture over the fruit. As you spread, some of the fruit pieces may partially show through the cheese layer; that's fine.
5.   With a kitchen mallet, crush the amaretti cookies and sprinkle the crumbs evenly over the cheese layer. Refrigerate for at least 2 hours.

NOTE: Italian sponge fingers are *low* fat, but not *no* fat; they are made with whole eggs. If you must (or if you cook for someone who must) avoid cholesterol altogether, do not use the sponge fingers. Bake the flat white Angel Sheet Cake (page 67) instead, and cut it into fingers. Use these virtually fat-free sponge fingers as the base for your extravaganza.

||||||||||||||||||||||||||||||||||||||||||||||||||||||||||||||||||||||||||||||||||

Fruit Ricotta Brûlée

SERVES 8
Per serving: 125.1 Cal. / 2.47 g fat / 18% fat / 8.00 mg cholesterol

Whip ricotta with orange marmalade and a whisper of vanilla and orange brandy, spread it over a mélange of berries and fruit, sprinkle with brown sugar, and broil until the sugar bubbles. When you chill the dish, the sugar hardens. Dipping your spoon through the hard sugar crust into the cream-covered fruit is pure pleasure.

½ pound sweet cherries, pitted and halved
2 ounces raspberries
8 ounces strawberries, hulled and halved
2 peaches, peeled, pitted, halved, and sliced
1 pound low-fat ricotta cheese
1 heaping tablespoon orange marmalade
1 teaspoon vanilla extract
1 tablespoon orange liqueur (Grand Marnier or Cointreau)
4 or 5 tablespoons light brown sugar

1. Preheat the oven to broil.
2. Arrange the fruit in an oblong 12-by-7-inch ovenproof ceramic baking dish. Cover and refrigerate while you prepare the topping.
3. Combine all the remaining ingredients except the brown sugar in the container of a food processor. Process until fluffy. Spoon and spread the mixture over the fruit.
4. Sprinkle the brown sugar evenly over the top and smooth with the back of spoon. Broil, close to the heat, ½ to 1 minute, until the sugar bubbles. Chill for at least 1 hour before serving.

CHOCOHOLICS UNITE

The Aztecs believed that Quetzalcoatl, the god of wind and fertility, presented cocoa to mankind. By all accounts Montezuma and his crowd consumed chocolate as a potent ceremonial drink made from cocoa paste, but the exact form of that drink is open to debate.

Both Columbus and Cortés, in the early sixteenth century, sent cocoa beans back to Spain. At first, chocolate was taken as a drink (as it would remain for 200 years), sweetened with sugar and flavored with vanilla. The English added milk to it in 1700. Toward the end of the eighteenth century French and Dutch processors found a way to defat the chocolate liquor and manufacture a powder. By the mid-nineteenth century, a solid eating chocolate was being manufactured by adding very finely ground sugar to cocoa butter. In 1876, milk chocolate was developed in Switzerland, and this became its most popular form.

Chocolate begins as cocoa beans encased in the pods of the cocoa tree; when the pods are ripe they are cut from the tree and chopped open. The beans and their surrounding pulp are piled into special boxes, covered with leaves, and left to ferment. Without fermentation the beans will not develop their characteristic and intoxicating chocolate aroma. Cocoa beans are very high in fat (cocoa butter). During processing the cocoa butter is removed. Later, it is put back, or, in some cases, vegetable fat is put back, and the cocoa butter is used for other things—cosmetics, for instance. Either way, solid chocolate has a high fat content. Even cocoa powder usually has fat returned to it. The fat content of cocoa powder can go as high as 25 percent.

Read the label of the cocoa you buy. Some brands can have a fat content as low as 14 to 15 percent. You may have to try a few brands to find the one that tastes best.

Chocolate Pudding

SERVES 4   MAKES 2 ¼ CUPS

Per serving: 123.1 Cal. / 0.68 g fat / 5% fat / 2.00 mg cholesterol

I cooked this low-fat chocolate pudding on BBC-TV, and it engendered more than 25,000 viewer responses. They had to hire extra secretaries to cope with the correspondence. This one is a winner!

4 tablespoons cocoa powder
4 tablespoons superfine sugar
2 tablespoons cornstarch
Tiny pinch of salt
2 cups skim milk

1. Put all the ingredients into the container of a blender, and blend until very smooth.
2. Rinse a heavy, nonstick saucepan with cold water. Pour out the water, but do not dry the saucepan (this helps reduce scorching). Pour the chocolate-milk mixture into the pan. Heat on medium, stirring, until it begins to bubble strenuously. As you stir do not scrape the bottom: If any scorching does occur on the bottom of the saucepan, you do not want to stir the scorched bits into the pudding. Continue stirring and cooking for 1 minute. Remove from the heat.
3. Immediately pour into glass dessert goblets. Cover with plastic wrap and refrigerate until serving time.

Chocolate "Butter"

MAKES 5 CUPS

Per tbsp.: 10.61 Cal. / 0.08 g fat / 6% fat / 0.12 mg cholesterol

This contains no butter, but it spreads like butter, and it will do delightfully wicked things to your slices of toast. It works exceptionally well as an icing or a filling for Layer Cake (page 68) or a Stir-Crazy Cake (pages 70–76). Substitute freshly brewed coffee for some of the liquid, and you have mocha "butter."

> *9 tablespoons cocoa powder*
> *3 tablespoons cornstarch*
> *5 tablespoons nonfat dry milk*
> *½ cup sugar*
> *½ teaspoon vanilla extract*
> *1½ cups skim milk*

1.   Sift the cocoa, cornstarch, dry milk, and sugar into a 2-quart microwave-safe plastic measuring cup.

2.   With a wire whisk, whisk the vanilla and milk into the dry ingredients. Whisk well; you don't want lumps. Cover the cup with plastic wrap.

3.   Microwave on high for 3 minutes (see Note). Uncover (avert your face and begin with the side *away* from you, to release the steam) and whisk thoroughly. Microwave on full power for 2 minutes more. Uncover and whisk again. Microwave for a further 1½ minutes, carefully uncover, and whisk. If necessary, microwave for another 1 or 2 minutes, until it is beautifully thickened, uncovering to whisk every 45 seconds. Uncover, whisk, and let stand for 5 minutes, whisking occasionally. Store with a covering of plastic wrap directly on the surface.

NOTE: These recipes have been tested with a 650-watt microwave oven. You will need to adjust the timing of the recipes to match the idiosyncrasies of your particular oven. Always jot down the cooking time after trying a recipe for the first time, so that there will be no need to guess next time.

Mocha "Butter"

MAKES 5 CUPS

Per tbsp.: 10.10 Cal. / 0.08 g fat / 6% fat / 0.10 mg cholesterol

9 tablespoons cocoa powder
3 tablespoons cornstarch
5 tablespoons nonfat dry milk
½ cup sugar

½ teaspoon vanilla extract
1 cup skim milk
½ cup cooled coffee (water-process decaf is fine, if you want
  to avoid caffeine)

1. Sift the cocoa, cornstarch, dry milk, and sugar into a 2-quart microwave-safe plastic measuring cup.
2. With a wire whisk, whisk the vanilla, milk, and coffee into the dry ingredients. Whisk well; you don't want lumps. Cover the cup with plastic wrap.
3. Microwave on full power for 3 minutes (see Note, page 164). Uncover (avert your face and begin with the side *away* from you, to release the steam) and whisk thoroughly. Cover again and microwave on full power for 2 minutes more. Uncover and whisk again. If the mixture hasn't boiled and thickened by now, microwave for another minute, then whisk again. If necessary, microwave for another ½ to 1 minute, until it is beautifully thickened. Uncover, whisk, and let stand for 5 minutes, whisking occasionally. Store with a covering of plastic wrap right on the surface.

Chocolate-Chestnut Pie

SERVES 8   MAKES ONE 10-INCH PIE
Per serving: 234.1 Cal. / 1.62 g fat / 6% fat / 0.32 mg cholesterol

Chestnuts are the only nuts that are low in fat, and chestnut purée is one of the all-time great carbohydrate foods in terms of texture and comfort. Chocolate and chestnut are natural partners, and in this two-tone pie, they achieve the perfect marriage. The bottom layer is chestnut-chocolate cream, the top layer is chocolate fudge with chestnut purée. If canned

||||||||||||||||||||||||||||||||||||||||||||||||||||||||||||||||||||||||||||||||

chestnut purée is not available where you live, it's fairly easy to make your own by puréeing canned whole chestnuts in the blender or food processor.

> *1 cup (8 ounces) unsweetened chestnut purée*
> *1 batch Hot Buttermilk Fudge Sauce, cooled (page 170)*
> *Granulated sugar substitute to taste (if needed)*
> *1 batch Chestnut-Chocolate Cream (page 170)*
> *1 Half-and-Half Crumb Crust (page 145), prepared in a*
> *   10-inch loose-bottomed pie pan*
> *Crumb garnish (pages 145–46)*

1.   In a food processor, combine the chestnut purée and fudge sauce and process until smooth and well blended. Taste the mixture. If you feel that it needs sweetening, blend in a bit of granulated sugar substitute.

2.   Swirl and spread the chestnut-chocolate cream over the crumb crust. Spread and swirl the fudge mixture over the chestnut cream. Sprinkle on the garnish. Cover and refrigerate for an hour or so.

3.   To serve, loosen around the edges, remove the sides of the pie pan, and cut the pie into wedges.

Chocolate-Almond Pie

S E R V E S   8

Per serving: 175.4 Cal. / 0.76 g fat / 4% fat / 1.47 mg cholesterol

Is it Valentine's Day? Your best friend's birthday? Do you have the urge to do something wonderful for someone you love? Perhaps the urge is to do something wonderful for *yourself.* Make this pie and bestow it tenderly upon those who need it.

Chocolate Pudding (page 162)
Amaretti Crumb Crust or Half-and-Half Crumb Crust (see
 pages 144–45)
1 amaretti cookie, crushed

Spread and swirl the chocolate pudding over the crust. Sprinkle the crushed amaretti over the top. Chill for several hours or overnight.

Chocolate Soufflé

SERVES 6

Per serving: 126.4 Cal. / 1.01 g fat / 7% fat / 0 mg cholesterol

Ignore rumors you may have heard about carob being a good substitute for chocolate. This soufflé is the real thing.

> *9 tablespoons superfine sugar*
> *9 tablespoons cocoa powder*
> *9 egg whites, at room temperature*
> *Pinch of cream of tartar*
> *1½ teaspoons vanilla extract*

1. Preheat the oven to 350° F. Remove the top oven shelf and set the other shelf in the center.
2. Sift together 7 tablespoons of the sugar with all of the cocoa. Set aside.
3. In an electric mixer, beat the egg whites with the cream of tartar until foamy. At highest speed, continue beating, adding the remaining 2 tablespoons of sugar a little at a time, until the whites hold stiff peaks.
4. With a rubber spatula, fold the sugar-cocoa mixture into the beaten whites. Fold in the vanilla.

5. Pile the mixture into a 3-quart soufflé dish. Bake in the center of the oven 30 to 40 minutes. Serve at once.

❚❚❚❚ VARIATION ❚❚❚❚

Fudgy Chocolate Torte: Use a 10-inch nonstick pie pan or quiche dish instead of a soufflé dish. Before baking, smooth the top with the back of a large spoon. Bake 30 to 35 minutes. If you bake it too long it will be dry. (A skewer inserted near the middle should emerge not quite clean.) Remove from the oven and let cool on a rack. Cut and serve right from the pan.

Chocolate Roulade

SERVES 10

Per serving: 99.22 Cal. / 0.80 g fat / 7% fat / 0.02 mg cholesterol

If the chocolate soufflé batter is baked flat on a paper-lined baking sheet, it becomes a base for a stunning roulade. Spread with a luxurious filling and then roll. It will leave your chocolate-loving friends speechless.

SOUFFLÉ BASE

> 9 tablespoons superfine sugar
> 9 tablespoons cocoa powder
> 9 egg whites, at room temperature
> Pinch of cream of tartar
> 1½ teaspoons vanilla extract
> 1½ teaspoons dark rum
> Confectioners' sugar

Chocolate "Butter" or Mocha "Butter" (page 163–65), Fig Butter (page 95), Chestnut-Chocolate Cream (recipe follows) or the topping from Tiramisù, Chocolate Tiramisù (pages 152 and 154), or the orange-ricotta tiramisù variation (page 153)

1. Preheat oven to 350° F.
2. Line a 9-by-13 inch nonstick baking sheet with baking parchment. Set aside.
3. Sift together 7 tablespoons of the sugar with all of the cocoa. Set aside.
4. In an electric mixer, beat the egg whites with the cream of tartar until foamy. At highest speed, continue beating, adding the remaining 2 tablespoons of sugar a little at a time, until the whites hold stiff peaks.
5. With a rubber spatula, fold the sugar-cocoa mixture into the beaten whites. Fold in the vanilla and rum.
6. Gently and evenly spread the mixture onto the prepared baking sheet. Bake for 18 to 22 minutes (a toothpick should test *almost* clean). Cool the pan on a rack.
7. Spread a clean dish towel on your work surface. Cover with a sheet of wax or greaseproof paper. Sprinkle evenly with confectioners' sugar. When the soufflé base is thoroughly cooled, turn it out onto the paper; peel off the baking parchment.
8. Spread with the filling of your choice. Starting from a long edge, roll the roulade base over the filling like a jelly roll, using the dish towel to help you roll. The cake may crack a bit, but that doesn't matter. Chill until needed. Serve in slices with Raspberry Coulis (page 124) if desired.

Chestnut-Chocolate Cream ♡🕐 ❄

MAKES 1 ½ CUPS

Per tbsp.: 18.14 Cal. / 0.16 g fat / 8% fat / 0.02 mg cholesterol

The perfect filling for a Chocolate Roulade (page 168), or one of the Stir-Crazy Layer Cakes (pages 70–76).

> 1 cup unsweetened chestnut purée
> ½ teaspoon vanilla extract
> 6 ounces fromage blanc, quark, or puréed nonfat cottage cheese
> 1 tablespoon sifted cocoa powder
> Approximately 2 tablespoons granulated sugar substitute, or to taste

Combine all the ingredients in the container of a food processor or blender. Process until thoroughly smooth and well mixed.

Hot Buttermilk Fudge Sauce ❄

MAKES 1 ¼ CUPS

Per tbsp.: 31.48 Cal. / 0.29 g fat / 8% fat / 0.11 mg cholesterol

This recipe, like the Chocolate "Butter" and the Chocolate-Almond Pie, the Deep Dark Chocolate Ice Cream, and the Chocolate Soufflé, has been designed for serious worshipers of the noble cocoa bean.

½ cup cocoa powder
½ cup superfine sugar
6 tablespoons nonfat dry milk
*2 tablespoons buttermilk powder (available from the baking
    department of the supermarket)*
½ cup cold water
1 teaspoon vanilla extract

1. Sift together the cocoa, sugar, dry milk, and buttermilk powder. Combine in the blender jar with the water and vanilla. Blend, stopping to scrape the sides, until well blended and perfectly smooth. Strain into a 2-quart microwave-safe plastic measuring cup. Cover tightly with plastic wrap.
2. Microwave on full power for 1 minute. *Carefully* uncover, (begin with the side away from you, and avert your face) and whisk well. Cover again and microwave for 30 seconds and whisk again. Cover and microwave for another 30 seconds. Uncover and whisk well. Use by the tablespoon as an ice cream topping, or chill, with plastic wrap right on the surface.

Chocolate Meringues

MAKES 60 COOKIES
Per cookie: 11.89 Cal. / 0.06 g fat / 5% fat / 0 mg cholesterol

Cream-filled chocolate cookies are a perennial favorite.

The method for making a healthy version couldn't be simpler. Prepare a batch of these meringues and a batch of Chocolate "Butter" (page 163) or Chestnut-Chocolate Cream (page 170), and introduce them to each other; that is to say, sandwich some of the butter or cream in between two meringues. Make this ½ to 1 hour before serving, to give the components a chance to marry. The meringue takes on a wonderful texture during the wait. But if you can't wait, slap them together and eat them at once.

> 3 egg whites, at room temperature
> Pinch of cream of tartar
> Pinch of salt
> ¾ cup sugar
> 1 teaspoon vanilla extract
> ⅓ cup cocoa powder, sifted

1. Preheat oven to 250° F.
2. Beat egg whites with cream of tartar and salt until foamy. Increase speed. Beat, adding sugar 1 or 2 tablespoons at a time, until shiny and stiff and firm peaks hold. Fold in vanilla and cocoa.
3. Line two baking sheets with parchment paper. Drop batter on sheets by the teaspoonful, 1 inch apart. Bake for 1½ hours.
4. Turn off oven. Leave cookies in the oven for 1 hour. Cool, then store in a cookie tin.

Chocolate Fondue

Chocolate fondue was invented in New York in the early sixties by a Swiss-American restaurateur named Conrad Egli. The happy news is that you can have a perfectly splendid Slim Cuisine chocolate fondue. Provide each diner with a vat of Hot Chocolate Sauce (page 121) or Chocolate Pudding (page 162), and with cubes of 1- or 2-day-old Angel Cake (page 65). If you wish, provide—in season—ripe strawberries as well. Spear, swirl, dunk, devour.

INDEX